PARTNERSHIP
OF PRINCIPLE

A

Also by Roy Jenkins
MR ATTLEE: *An Interim Biography*
PURSUIT OF PROGRESS
MR BALFOUR'S POODLE
SIR CHARLES DILKE: *A Victorian Tragedy*
THE LABOUR CASE
ASQUITH
ESSAYS AND SPEECHES
AFTERNOON ON THE POTOMAC
WHAT MATTERS NOW
NINE MEN OF POWER

PARTNERSHIP OF PRINCIPLE

Writings and Speeches on the
Making of the Alliance
by
ROY JENKINS

Selected and Edited
by
CLIVE LINDLEY

Published by the Radical Centre
in association with
Secker & Warburg, London

First published in Great Britain 1985
by The Radical Centre
Sellarsbrooke Park, Ganarew,
Monmouth, Gwent NP5 3SS
in association with
Martin Secker & Warburg Limited
54 Poland Street, London W1V 3DF

British Library Cataloguing in Publication Data

Jenkins, Roy
Partnership of principle: writings and speeches on the making of the Alliance.
1. Liberal Party 2. Social Democratic Party   I. Title   II. Lindley, Clive   III. Radical Centre 324 24106   JN1129.L42

ISBN 0-436-22100-4 (Hbk)
ISBN 0-436-22101-2 (Pbk)

Typesetting by Reprodux Printers Ltd., Hereford
Printed in Great Britain by Polyploy Ltd. in association with Reprodux

CONTENTS

Editor's Preface
Author's Introduction

PART ONE: THE BIRTH OF THE ALLIANCE

PART TWO: GENERAL PRINCIPLES

EDITOR'S PREFACE

Eighteen years ago *Essays and Speeches* by Roy Jenkins was published by Collins, edited by Anthony Lester. Roy Jenkins, then aged 47, was about to become Chancellor of the Exchequer — Alan Watkins' admirable book *Brief Lives* tells us that Margaret Thatcher thought him the best Chancellor since 1945.

He had already served his first term as Home Secretary (1965 - 67) after other Ministerial appointments. He was, by any political standards, an outstanding success. As a distinguished biographer and historian he had published books on Asquith, Dilke, Attlee and Balfour. He was to serve a second term at the Home Office and was, for a time, Deputy Leader of the Labour Party. In 1976 he left the House of Commons, and seemingly British politics, to take up the appointment of President of the Commission of the European Community.

From 1967 until January 1981, when his European appointment ended, he made a number of speeches, gave lectures and wrote many articles. Towards the end of that period one speech was of particular importance in the context of British politics. It was, of course, his Dimbleby Memorial Lecture delivered for the BBC in November 1979: 'Home Thoughts from Abroad'. Six years later I believe that nothing in his distinguished earlier career, either in Britain or in Europe, compares in terms of historical importance with the events that stemmed from that BBC Television lecture.

The British political community buzzed with anticipation as the 1980s dawned. Seven months later, in June 1980, Roy Jenkins again spoke in Britain. He was the guest of the Parliamentary Press Gallery. Then this former Minister of Aviation talked in terms of launching an experimental plane. After that everybody knew what he intended but many had reservations as to whether such a fundamental re-shaping of the British party political system could succeed.

Some years later, attending a Council for Social Democracy meeting at Aston University in Birmingham, on a Sunday afternoon when press, television and radio reporters had disappeared, I heard Roy Jenkins, no longer Leader of SDP, deliver a masterly though short speech. In just fifteen minutes he outlined the issues of defence and disarmament and the SDP approach to them. It seemed to me that such a brilliant distillation of fact and perception should reach a wider audience than the four hundred or so of my Council colleagues who were present. As the idea took hold, I realised that modern political history and the topography of the recent political landscape could be coherently traced by reference to the speeches and articles of Roy Jenkins.

There is another sense in which I believe this collection of writings, lectures and speeches is worth publishing. Roy Jenkins is the principal architect of a new order in British politics but he is also one of the last of the tradition of classical platform orators that have so distinguished the British political scene. In a period marked by technological innovations in communications, it seems more and more likely that political leaders will be judged by three-minute television appearances and their ability to stand up to interrogation at press conferences. The public confrontations of the future seem destined to be of a Presidential nature, with each party's best television performer battling for the electoral ratings, in two-dimensional appearance in the corner of millions of British sitting rooms.

The day of the platform performance is almost over, with only by-elections providing a forum for masters of the art of oratory. But public meetings have played a very significant part in the formation of the SDP and the building of the Alliance, as perhaps this book will demonstrate.

In selecting and editing this collection, I have delighted, once again, in the combination of clarity of thought, authority of prescription and the elegant prose in which it is expressed. All of these characteristics exemplify the stature of the author.

As a supporter, and self-appointed aide between the Dimbleby Lecture and the launch of the SDP, and thereafter a minor colleague, I make no pretence of impartiality in the connecting passages (printed in italics) which I have contributed. The speeches themselves delineate the passage of events.

My thanks are due to *The Times, The Financial Times, The Guardian, New Democrat* magazine, and the Cambridge Liberal Association for permission to quote material in which they hold the copyright.

July 1985   **Clive Lindley**

AUTHOR'S INTRODUCTION

Clive Lindley surprised me a few months ago by suggesting that he would like to arrange publication of a selection of my speeches going back to the gestation and birth of the SDP. This obviously involved my re-reading them. There is little that I wish unsaid. I am happy for them to be published, and maybe even read. But we are too young a Party for nostalgia. 1987 will be a still more important year for the SDP and the Alliance than was 1981.

How valid do the assumptions of 1981 remain? What were they? In the first couple of years of life of the Thatcher Government I thought that the most likely result of the next General Election would be the return to office of the Labour Party. The pendulum would swing away from the Government as it had done on each occasion since 1959, except for the two quick elections, that of 1966 and the second one of 1974, and the dreary business of re-nationalising what had been de-nationalised and reversing most other policies in sight would begin all over again. 'Queasy rides on the idealogical big dipper', in the phrase I had used in the Dimbleby Lecture, had been turning the stomach of British industry — and of other forms of national activity — for too long. Governments of the Right were as responsible as governments of the Left. They each produced several industries to mess about with, a new pensions scheme, a different board to deal with prices or incomes or 'lame ducks'. The primary result was that the British economy operated in a much less stable political framework than did the economies of all her main competitors. The secondary result was that while the British Governments could and did deliver plenty of impermanent and unwanted legislation none of them could deliver the main benefit they promised, which was sustained economic growth. Disillusionment therefore came early with successive governments, and the rancid oil which this produced kept the swinging pendulum only too well lubricated.

That looked likely to continue. The crassness of the Labour Party in electing Mr Foot as leader and making a constitutional nonsense at the unfortunate Wembley Conference did not lead to a collapse of electoral support. On the contrary, the party had a strong opinion poll lead in the first half of 1981 and scored great gains in the County Council elections that May. I had left the Labour Party not because I feared it could not be elected, but because, with its new policies, I did not want it to be elected. A few undesirable manifesto policies are clearly par for the course in most forms of party politics, particularly two-party politics. But no self-respecting Social Democrat could possibly swallow a combination of withdrawal from Europe, unilateralism, the effective destruction of NATO, economic autarchy, large-scale nationalisation, the prohibition by law of non-state education or medicine, single chamber government, and a vastly inflationary budget policy. This was the diet which the 1981-3 Labour Party offered to the British electorate. To have advocated support for it would have been a sign not of robust political digestion but of an indifference to the interests of the country.

The Labour Party had therefore to be stopped. It had deserted sense. It had to be shown that power had deserted it. In the early days there was no great difficulty about achieving this result. Mrs Thatcher seems to have had an extraordinary illusion that the SDP has taken votes only from the Conservative Party. Whatever may be the case in the future, that has certainly not been true in the past. It was the Labour Party which received the worst shock at Warrington; it was the Labour vote which totally collapsed at Crosby; and it was the Labour Party which, in my view, would have won Hillhead without us. But more important than these early skirmishes was the outcome of the 1983 General Election. The incontrovertible fact is that a divided opposition then gave Mrs Thatcher a ridiculously high return of seats for votes. Mr Heath in 1966 had to be content with 253 seats for almost exactly the same proportion of the total vote which, in 1983, gave Mrs Thatcher 396.

Nevertheless 1983 was in some real sense a Thatcher victory. Psychologically, even if not arithmetically, it was more than a victory by default. Her self-confidence was high. Her dominance of the Conservative Party was total. Her hold on at any rate a large minority of the British public, was almost hypnotic.

That high noon looks to be over. There is a new uncertainty of touch about the Government. In the first term Mrs Thatcher at least gave the impression of knowing where she was going. Now there are many lurches, sudden foolish initiatives, half-pursued and then abandoned under pressure.

However, I only say 'looks to be over'. The experience of 1981-82 must teach us the political lesson that unpopular Prime Ministers are not necessarily beyond the hope of recovery. Nevertheless, it is difficult to see a new Falklands, and still more significantly stridency is coming to grate, even on the Conservative Party, and self-righteousness is beginning to bore. And it is more difficult for a relationship to recover from boredom than from hostility.

A wide window of opportunity therefore opens for the second time before the Alliance. Brecon and Radnor was a very significant by-election. It was the first one in this Parliament which started as a genuine three-horse race. We had to beat off a strong and effective Labour challenge, and do it from a position of being third to their second in 1983. And, to put it mildly, there was no question of the public opinion polls creating a bandwagon effect for us.

There are both similarities with, and differences from, 1981, when such a prospect previously offered itself. Then as now the Prime Minister and the Government were unpopular. Then as now, but not in the intervening period, the Labour Party was in a position from which it could conceivably win. But then the Government was giving no sense of having run its course. On the other hand the Labour Party, then much more than now, was clearly poised to embrace fresh bursts of lunacy.

The SDP itself had all the enthusiasm and inexperience of extreme youth. It had little behind it but a buoyant sense of adventure and widespread aspirations which had long been waiting to be tapped. It was not battle-trained. It could make a triumphant swoop but it knew nothing about digging in or picking itself up and fighting again after setback or defeat. The Alliance was even newer. It had just had an almost accidentally arranged but extremely enthusiastic honeymoon at Llandudno. In this first flush we soared up in the polls to positions even higher than those we achieved in the polling booths of our extremely successful by-elections. Late that autumn they all put us overwhelmingly in the lead. One gave us over fifty per cent, with the other half of the electorate split almost equally between Labour and Conservatives. Landslide victories were predicted.

Obviously this full headiness could not last. It turned down quickly and before the Falklands war. Already in March 1982 Hillhead was a more difficult campaign to fight than Warrington had been eight months before. Quite a difficult year then followed and for a variety of reasons we did not get a flying start into the 1983 election. We were only around 20 per cent in the polls when the date was announced. We put on five points during the campaign, and achieved an outcome of 25.4 per cent. It was not sensational, indeed disappointing against the hopes of 1981, but it was, I believe, the highest total ever achieved by a new grouping without the upheaval of a change of regime, in any democracy.

There is now the basis, more solid than in 1981, from which we can in 1987, provided we play our hand correctly, achieve the full breakthrough which had narrowly evaded us. It is more solid because, although less flushed with the first enthusiasm, we are better organised, more experienced and manifestly permanent. There is also every prospect of starting the next election campaign ten points ahead of where we began in 1983. From that position all possibilities are within our grasp.

'Playing our hand correctly' involves three main precepts. First, we must underpin our Alliance with the Liberals in every possible way. Above all this means accepting and welcoming its permanence. The achievement of electoral reform (not itself an easy task) would in no way lessen the need for the Alliance. Under no electoral system will there be room in the hearts of the British people for more than three mainstream political groups. Indeed any thought that the new system would encourage us to split would discourage its achievement, for there are many who would like a fairer and more rational system but who fear fragmentation. Once permanence is totally established most other internal problems of the Alliance will fall into place. Even fusion can be considered calmly and rationally, neither hurried nor recoiled from.

Second, we must set up no limit to the bounds of our success. Nothing is certain, but starting from thirty per cent or above we can achieve a dominant position in the next Parliament. We should campaign at least for power not balance.

Third, we must be clear about the political orientation of our party. In the early days, paradoxically it seems to me now, I was probably considered to be the most right-wing of the Gang of Four. It is true that I was least frightened of the 'centre' party concept (although I never much liked the actual word), that I had least desire to cling to the socialist label, which I thought had long since become at best obfuscating rather than clarifying, and that I had least desire to pretend to membership of the Socialist International, which I saw as a club that, *pace* Groucho Marx, wanted us as little as we needed to join. Nor did I ever fear that the Liberal alliance could draw us to the Right. But I always saw the SDP as being a radical alternative to the Tories, a left-of-centre party if the old hemicycle terms are to be used.

This is particularly important today. Post-Thatcher the country will not want a sub-Thatcherite alternative. A lot of nonsense is also talked about her having uniquely changed the intellectual climate of politics in a way to which everyone will have to adjust. Any prime minister who holds office for any length of time changes the political climate. Baldwin did. Attlee did. Lord Stockton did. But that does not mean that what was good sense when they started had to be discounted before they had finished. And in many ways all of them achieved more measurable benefits than Mrs Thatcher has done.

In 1987 the easier task for the Alliance will be to eat into Conservative votes: apart from anything else there are more of them. That meal will be desirable and wholesome. But if it were almost our sole diet the result could well be the return of a majority (in terms of seats) Labour Government sustained perhaps by thirty-five per cent of those voting or twenty-four per cent of the electorate. That would be neither desirable nor wholesome, except insofar as it provided a good sharp lesson for the Tory excoriators of proportional representation. But it would be an expensive one. It is much better that we should keep our radical edge well-honed and endeavour to cut as deep in Durham as in Devon.

16 June 1985   **Roy Jenkins**

PART ONE

THE BIRTH OF THE ALLIANCE

CHAPTER I

The Beginning

Home Thoughts from Abroad

*This speech, delivered as the 1979 Dimbleby Lecture, could be called the
beginning of the beginning. It offered Roy Jenkins's analysis of current ills
and an abundance of signals, signposts, assertions and conclusions.*

*Jenkins as the President of the Commission of the EEC was temporarily
divorced from British party politics. In 1979, politics in Britain had
polarised at the extremes of left and right ideology; between the defeated
Labour Party and the triumphant Tories. In retrospect, it is hard to see who
else in public life could have delivered such a political analysis and set out
the possible alternatives without it being a party political speech in
favour of one of the established parties.*

*From that time on, a critical path was established leading inevitably to the
foundation of the SDP, the Alliance with the Liberals, and the replacement
of the pendulum by the tripod as the mechanism of British politics. To many
disenchanted moderates in the Labour Party, the Dimbleby Lecture led to
their reincarnation as Social Democrats based on European models,
rather than Socialists a word now so traduced as to be descriptively
useless.*

*To many people with no political affiliations, the Arctic of Labour and the
Antarctic of Thatcherism were equally hostile environments. The Dimbleby
Lecture gave them hope that the future would not for ever be dominated by
these warring ideologies.*

My title of 'Home Thoughts From Abroad' is not perhaps wholly
informative. What I want to talk about is the state of British politics
today, not primarily the parties or individual politicians, but the system
itself, and whether and how it ought to be changed and improved. I start
with some historical analysis and then attempt to say how and why I
think we could escape from what I increasingly regard as the constricting
rigidity — almost the tyranny — of the present party system.

After over twenty-eight years in the House of Commons and nine years
as a Minister, I have been mostly in Brussels for the past three years. Such
separation has not diminished my interest in what goes on here —
perhaps less so than I expected at the start — nor my belief that we retain
great potential in Britain, and that the barrier which prevents us from
turning it into national success is a narrow one. I speak purely personally,

not in my present official capacity, but on the basis of experience and reflection stemming from half a lifetime in British politics.

The British political system in broadly its present form is just about a hundred years old. Over this span of a century Britain has changed enormously, perhaps even more than most other Western countries. Externally it was the richest and most powerful country in the world, commanding an empire unparalleled in human history. Now it lies twentieth, and falling, in the tables of national wealth per head. And the empire has gone with the speed of soft snow under a warm, damp westerly wind. Internally there have been vast shifts in the balance of social and economic power. We were then an exceptionally deferential society compared with, say, either America or France, and Britain was not only renowned for its national riches but a few Englishmen were renowned for their personal wealth and lavish way of life. Now the deference has gone, and we have become more renowned abroad for our parsimony than for our opulence.

Yet all this change has happened within the skin of a political system which has in its essentials remained the same. That is exceptional. Almost every other major country has changed its basic system, some of them several times. Traditionally this British stability was considered a major national asset. Now the question is whether the stability has not turned into political rigidity, whether the old skin is not now drawn too tight for effective national performance.

As that national performance has become increasingly disappointing, so there has developed an increasing tendency to criticise the political framework within which it has flagged, and the somewhat ossified form which this hundred-year-old model has now assumed.

This brings me to why I chose to put that as its approximate age. The year 1868 marked the end of a confused period of mid-nineteenth century politics and the election of the first Gladstone Government. Hitherto governments had mostly emerged from shifting combinations in the House of Commons, with royal preference playing a significant role. Although this was not immediately apparent, a new pattern then began to emerge.

Henceforth the general election was the key factor, and governments assumed a much sharper party shape. The House of Commons, as a selector of governments, faded into the background. It long retained its position as a gladiatorial arena, in which individual reputations were made or lost, but that was different from making governments.

Thus British government became essentially party government. Despite the significance I have attached to the 1868 date the system did not spring fully grown from the sea. It took many decades to evolve into its full rigidity. Many MPs occupied semi-independent positions. The great majority were, of course, financially independent — they had to be, with no parliamentary salaries until 1911; they did not depend greatly upon national machines or even national policies for their votes; quite a lot were consistently returned unopposed; and a good many were without political ambition, beyond that of being a member of the House of Commons. The power of the party whips was therefore very limited. The House of Commons might not have much power to make or break governments, but it was nobody's poodle.

The position persisted broadly until the 1920s. The major factor of change then was the rise of the Labour Party. The degree of independence which had softened the corners of the party system was an independence largely based on class. Once a working-class party arose — although there were always strong middle-class elements in the Labour Party — most of the factors I have just described obviously ceased to apply. Furthermore the Labour Party had a strong strand of 'democratic centralism' in its theory — although probably more in its theory than in its practice. It believed in discipline, in the importance of the party conference, in the idea of the mandate, of a government being elected to carry out a detailed and specific programme which it had announced in advance.

Between the wars politics were unbalanced. The Labour Party had achieved a remarkable feat in breaking through the defences of the system to replace the Liberal Party. But it had done so at the price of two decades of Conservative dominance. After 1945 the balance was restored. In the twenty-one years from 1918 to 1939 there were only three years when the Conservatives were not in office. In the thirty-four years since 1945 each major party has had seventeen of government. The post-war period should therefore have been the apotheosis of the two-party system. Superficially it has worked with smoothness and with perfect fairness. But has it?

It began well. The Attlee Government is now widely regarded as a great administration. It was the first major reforming government since that of 1905. It changed the map of the world and it changed the social map of Britain. Very few of its major measures have been reversed. It did not do so without provoking division in the country. But that division was well within the confines of constitutional tolerance and was less indeed than that provoked by the Asquith administration before 1914.

Although after the excitements of Churchill's wartime administration it was sometimes accused of being a drab government, presiding over a drab period, it did not bore the electorate. It infuriated part of it, but it produced no alienation from politics, no disenchantment with the two big parties.

On the contrary it led to two of the most remarkable general elections ever seen. At the first in 1950 the Labour Government just hung on. At

B

the second in 1951 the Conservatives just scraped home. But what was remarkable was the high degree of participation in both, the command of the two major parties over their great armies of supporters, and the uniformity of the pattern of results from constituency to constituency, from region to region. They were the two great mass plebiscites of British electoral history.

Members who did not wear one or other of the great party labels were nearly obliterated. Before the dissolution in 1950 there were thirty-seven independents or members of third parties. After the 1951 election there were nine. The British 'first past the post' system had always been hard on those unanointed by the two major parties, but before 1950 this had been mitigated in a number of ways. Now the juggernauts were supreme, but it did not much matter at the time because it was so obviously in accord with the electoral mood of the country. In 1951 the most strict system of proportional representation would have given the Liberals only fifteen seats against the six which they secured.

The new Conservative Government was also successful. It relaxed the acerbities of Crippsian austerity without undoing the core of the work of the Attlee administration. The economy, responding to greater freedom and favourable terms of trade, did well for several years. At the 1955 election the Conservatives increased their tiny majority, but in no way sensationally. The big parties retained their dominance.

Britain up to this point seemed to have been dealing reasonably successfully with the post-war world. We were still third in the hierarchy of world power. We were still substantially richer than either France or Germany.

Then came two major events. The first, short and sharp, was Suez. The second was the formation of the European Economic Community (EEC) without our participation. The first was our last imperial adventure, and shatteringly unsuccessful. It was the end of our pretension to be an independent world power. Thereafter, as long as the American *imperium* lasted, we cleaved close to Washington.

The effect on the French, who had been involved with us in the Suez débâcle, was quite different. We turned across the Atlantic. They turned across the Rhine, and Europe was built without us. There is room for argument about the causes of what followed. There is no doubt about what happened. Over the first thirteen years of the Community's life national income per head increased by seventy-two per cent in the Six and by thirty-five per cent in Britain. The result was that from being almost the richest country in Western Europe we became one of the poorest. France for the first time since the industrial revolution surpassed us in economic strength. The German economy achieved nearly twice our weight.

The British people responded uneasily to these setbacks. We did not, of course, go around with national income statistics in our pockets, pulling them out and pondering over them in pubs. But we had a nasty feeling that things were not going well. And this came on top of the bumpy psychological adjustment to the loss of an empire and a world rôle.

British governments responded in two ways. First they made intermittent efforts to get into the European Community. But once we wantonly had missed the initial opportunity, when we would have been universally welcomed, this was not easy. We were twice blocked. It took us until 1973, and then, by a singular misfortune, the great European surge to prosperity had exhausted itself. We were only allowed to use our surfboard when the waves were dying, at least temporarily.

Second, and perhaps more important from the point of view of the evolution of the British political system, new governments became more and more enthusiastic in promising the one thing they could not deliver: a higher rate of economic growth that would enable us to catch up. The more the secret of higher productivity and a dynamic economy eluded us, the more the search dominated each election campaign. But not, on the part of politicians, in a mood of questioning humility. The opposition party of the day always believed it had the philosopher's stone. Elect us, they — including myself — said, and the economy will bound forward. Quite often they were elected, but the economy did nothing of the sort. The result was a widening gap between promise and performance.

It was not that governments could do nothing. They could nationalise or denationalise industries at the drop of a hat — or at any rate at the drop of a parliamentary guillotine. They could replace one body to deal with prices or incomes or both with another under a different name and in a slightly different form.

They could introduce one pension scheme and then see it replaced by another — marginally better or marginally worse — within a few years, and that in turn replaced by a third one when there had been another swing of the political pendulum. The trouble was that most of these changes exacerbated rather than cured the fundamental economic ill, and irritated rather than satisfied the mass of the electorate.

This showed itself in several ways. There was a decline in the active membership of the parties. There was a decline in the participation in elections, and there was a decline within that reduced participation in the share of the votes going to the big parties. In 1951 eighty-three per cent of the electorate voted, and no less than ninety-seven per cent of those who went to the polls voted for one or other of the two big parties. In the second 1974 election only seventy-three per cent of the electorate voted, and only three-quarters of those — as opposed to the ninety-seven per cent in 1951 —voted Labour or Conservative. To put it another way: the

Labour Party in 1951 polled forty per cent of the total electorate, including those who stayed at home, and it just lost. In October 1974 it polled twenty-eight per cent of the electorate and it just won. Even in 1979, with some recovery in the total vote and a substantial victory, the Conservatives polled only thirty-three per cent of the electorate.

Another sign of disillusion was the growing habit of governments to lose support almost as soon as they had been elected. The Labour Government of 1945 lost not a single by-election in its six years of office. The Conservative Government of 1951 actually gained one by-election and lost none. Thereafter the pattern changed. Every subsequent government sustained swingeing by-election defeats. The Conservatives quite often lost to the Liberals, the Labour Party mainly to the Conservatives or to a nationalist candidate. But from 1958 to 1978 the safest seats were liable to topple.

This represented no settled view on the part of the electorate. The seats often returned to their previous allegiance at the subsequent general election. But for most of its period of office every government, on the evidence of by-elections and public opinion polls alike, looked unpopular and bereft. This was inevitably damaging to its authority and consistency of purpose.

There has also been a weakening of the position of the House of Commons. It has recently declined as a forum of national debate, or even as a gladiatorial arena in which political reputations are made or destroyed, on top of its long-lost government-making capacity.

We are therefore confronted with a somewhat depressing balance sheet; a political system which previously served us well, but which has recently become stranded by the receding tide of public commitment; a House of Commons which should be its chief ornament, but which commands diminishing respect; and an inadequate national performance, which may be due to entirely different reasons but which certainly gives no basis for complacency about the framework in which it has declined.

What can and should be done? How, over the next decade, could we improve the form and content of British politics, make them more representative of and more responsive to the aspirations of the public, and in the process perhaps help to secure that desperately needed recovery of the British economy and of British national self-confidence?

There are two main aspects. First, there is the content of politics; second there is the institutional form, although the two obviously interact upon each other.

On the content we must try to lengthen our perspective, and escape from the tyranny of the belief, against all the evidence, that one government can make or break us.

A few decades ago there were quite a lot of people who believed that a single election victory could be the beginning of the millennium. It was a view perhaps more prevalent, because of greater optimism or utopianism, on the Left than on the Right. It was certainly held by many Labour supporters in 1945. More recently, however, I have the impression that it applies equally or more strongly on the right.

A governing party must have the self-confidence to want power and to believe that its exercise of it can tilt the country in the right direction. But it should also have the humility to recognise on any likely projection of the past, its power will come to an end, probably in about six years, maybe less, only exceptionally more. The test of its statesmanship in the context of history will not therefore be how many trees it pulls up by the roots but how it fits into a continuous process of adaptation in which leadership is combined with sensitivity to national mood.

We may or may not have too much legislation, but we certainly have too much short-lived legislation, measures put on the statute book by one party in the almost certain knowledge that they will be reversed by the other. This could be avoided if governments, before embarking on a major controversial bill, would ask themselves one simple question: is it likely to last? If it is, do it with conviction. If not, please spare us too many queasy rides on the ideological big dipper.

This is not a recipe for inaction or for the avoidance of controversy. Some of the most bitterly contested measures of the past 150 years — the electoral reform bills, the repeal of the Corn Laws, the curbing of the powers of the House of Lords, the initiation of social security, or, to take an example from the Right, the setting up of independent television — have been inviolate once they were on the statute book because they quickly became part of the social fabric and could only have been undone at the cost of unacceptable electoral damage to the opposing party.

All this implies a certain respect by politicians for the opinions of their opponents. But that is surely both possible and desirable. In their memoirs, written with the benignity of old age, it generally comes through. Indeed, where bitterness remains, it is more often directed against previous colleagues than against previous opponents.

Yet when they are seeking or exercising power there is only too often a shrill and unconvincing attempt to portray almost everyone on the other side as either a fool or a knave. Each successive Tory government is the most reactionary since that of Lord Liverpool, or some other hobgoblin figure shrouded in the past. Each successive Labour government has been the most rapacious, doctrinaire and unpatriotic conspiracy to be seen this side of the Iron Curtain. Either might, I suppose, be true in the future, but it cannot all have been true in the past, and I do not believe that it either convinces or pleases the electorate.

One major disadvantage of excessive political partisanship is that it fosters precisely the sort of industrial mood which is rapidly turning Britain into a manufacturing desert. If, on the House of Commons floor, it is always the fault of the other side, how can politicians preach convincingly against the prevalence of such a mood on the shop-floor?

This, some people will say with horror, is an unashamed plea for the strengthening of the political centre. Why not? The vocation of politicians ought to be to represent, to channel, to lead the aspirations of the electorate. These aspirations, not on every issue, but in essential direction, pull far more towards the centre than towards the extremes. The general mood is not that of reaction or of putting the clock back. But nor is it one of support for class selfishness or for revolution, whether it be utopian or malevolent.

Now, institutional questions. I believe that the case for proportional representation is overwhelming. The main argument for it lies in refuting the main argument against it. This may sound negative, but it is not —and for this reason. It is clearly a fairer system, accepted as such by the great majority of democratic countries. The onus of proof must be upon those who wish to defend the existing system under which you give only a handful of parliamentary seats to twenty per cent or even twenty-five per cent of the electorate. And as there is a greater alienation from the two big parties it has become more indefensible. And as it becomes more indefensible, so the alienation feeds upon itself.

Traditionally the obvious case in equity was in Britain defeated by three considerations. First it could be said that it was only a little inequity, because, as in 1950 and 1951, the overwhelming majority seemed happy voting for and working with one or other of the big parties. As the numbers voting for those parties, and perhaps even more dramatically, those enthusiastically working for them has fallen, so this argument has collapsed.

Second, there has been a simple 'what we have we hold' approach by the established parties. Why let anyone we do not have to get their nose into the trough of political power? This has never been very creditable, but it must be said that it has motivated not only the Conservative and Labour Parties but also the Liberal Party in its long period of power. And it was made more respectable by the third argument: that it worked; that it produced strong, effective, coherent government; that it avoided the weakness of incompatible coalitions between parties, and made our system the envy of the world; and that this was more important than abstract equity.

But where stands that argument today? Effective, coherent government? Do we really believe that we have been more effectively and coherently governed over the past two decades than have the Germans, with their very sensible system of proportional representation?

The avoidance of incompatible coalitions? Do we really believe that the last Labour Government was not a coalition, in fact if not in name, and a pretty incompatible one at that? I served in it for half its life, and you could not convince me of anything else.

Coalitions got a bad name in England partly because of a superficial aphorism by Disraeli, and partly because the word became associated with the worst phase of Lloyd George's career and with the 'hard-faced men' who then supported him. But some form of coalition is essential for democratic leadership. Roosevelt established a broad coalition of interest which underpinned the American Democratic Party for fifty years. The old Labour Party of Attlee and Gaitskell was a coalition of liberal social democrats and industrially responsible trades unionists. Willy Brandt and Helmut Schmidt have governed the Federal Republic of Germany with a coalition of Social Democrats and Liberals for the past decade. Sometimes the coalitions are overt, sometimes they are covert. I do not think the distinction greatly matters. The test is whether those within the coalition are closer to each other, and to the mood of the nation they seek to govern, than they are to those outside their ranks.

I am therefore unfrightened by the argument against proportional representation that it would probably mean frequent coalitions — although not across the whole board of politics. I would much rather that it meant overt and compatible coalition than that it locked incompatible people, and still more important, incompatible philosophies, into a loveless, constantly bickering and debilitating marriage, even if consecrated in a common tabernacle.

The great disadvantage of our present electoral system is that it freezes the pattern of politics, and holds together the incompatible because everyone assumes that if a party splits it will be electorally slaughtered. They may be right. They may be wrong. I am not so sure. I believe that the electorate can tell 'a hawk from a handsaw' and that if it saw a new grouping with cohesion and relevant policies it might be more attracted by this new reality than by old labels which had become increasingly irrelevant.

But the possibility that a break out *might* now succeed does not invalidate the argument that the present system militates too much against a shift in the pattern, makes the moderates too much the prisoners of the extremists.

Let us examine briefly two other common arguments against proportional representation. First it is not true that it must produce a great multiplicity of tiny splinter parties. The German system by which you have to get five per cent of the national votes to qualify for a national seat is an effective barrier against this. They have operated stably with three parties for decades. Here there might be four or five, which is much what we have now. But the balance between them would be far more fairly struck.

Second, it is suggested, was indeed suggested by Lord Hailsham in one of the most distinguished in this series of lectures, that it might encourage extremist parties, a big Communist Party or even a Fascist Party. I do not follow that argument. Italy, admittedly, has proportional representation and a big Communist Party. But the one is not the cause of the other. Indeed, if the British electoral system prevailed in Italy, the Communists might well have more and not fewer seats.

France also has a big Communist Party, but does *not* have proportional representation. Germany, with proportional representation, has a negligible Communist Party. Much the same applies in Holland, Belgium, Ireland, Denmark, Sweden. In Britain proportional representation would, in my view, be likely to give a small bloc of seats to a party of the far left, although not to the Communist Party as such. But this overt result would be far more reasonable than allowing much the same people to have a sizeable say in the choice of candidates and the manifesto on which they fight in up to three hundred seats.

Nothing is perfect, and nothing, of course, solves everything. Nor will we get electoral reform overnight. In the meantime we should consider what other changes of political method we need both while waiting for the change of system and to buttress it when it comes. A great argument has been joined about democracy within the Labour Party. It is an important subject, with political and constitutional implications extending well beyond the domestic affairs of one party. But to some considerable extent the basis for it appears to me to be misconceived. The questions are wrongly posed. It is desirable neither to stand rigidly upon the *status quo* nor to hand over still greater power to an unrepresentative party machine whose pretensions on policy become greater as its effectiveness in maintaining a powerful organisation in the country — the real job of a party machine — becomes less.

This applies to most of the issues in dispute. Should it be made easier to get rid of sitting MPs? No one should argue that an MP, however ineffective his performance, is entitled to a plush-covered seat for life. But equally there is no real democracy, or respect for representative parliamentary government, in suggesting that tiny groups of perhaps twenty or thirty activists should have power of political life or death over a member who has been elected by 20,000 or 30,000 constituents and whose fault is not lack of personal effectiveness but the advocacy of political views which are probably much closer to those of the 20,000 or 30,000 than to those of the 'people's court' of the twenty or thirty. 'Who can tell for certain?', it may be rejoined. Indeed. Then let it be put to the test. Let there be the full right for an MP to be challenged. But let it be done before those to whom he ought to be responsible — the mass of his electorate. Either give the MP reasonable security to get on with his job, or if a major dispute arises with his local party, let a properly organised and officially conducted *primary election* be held.

Equally the disputes about who should elect the party leader and who should prepare the party manifesto raise wider questions than can be solved by a simple defensive battle.

There is a lot to be said for a potential leader's parliamentary colleagues having a dominant say in the choice. But he is also intended to be the leader of the whole party, and there is nothing inherently shocking in the view that some wider electoral college should be involved. Such a system has produced the best as well as the worst American presidents, and it is the way in which most European political leaders are chosen. What is peculiar is the assumption that in the present-day Labour Party another form of election would be likely to produce a result unacceptable to the majority of the Labour MPs. This, of course, is what gives the issue interest. So with the manifesto. It is not a question of whether the better polemical stylists are in Transport House or in the Parliamentary Labour Party. It is that the National Executive Committee would wish to write a totally different sort of manifesto, one on which the majority of those now elected by the people would not wish to fight, and on which they do not believe they could govern even if elected. Nothing could be more calculated to stretch still further the already dangerous gap between the promises and the performance of British governments.

The wider question that is raised is therefore the previous one of the inherent incompatibility of a party in which every demarcation dispute is an idealogical one, in which, to paraphrase A.E. Housman's 'The Welsh Marches',

> *They cease not fighting, left and right,*
> *On the marches of my breast.*

This is not to argue against some dispute and tension within parties being inevitable and indeed desirable. Such reasonable and creative tension is however a far cry from a position in which internecine warfare is the constant and major purpose of a party's life. The response to such a situation, in my view, should not be to slog through an unending war of attrition, stubbornly and conventionally defending as much of the old citadel as you can hold, but to break out and mount a battle of movement on new and higher ground.

There is an important subsidiary point. If you remain in a beleaguered citadel you must necessarily look for a relieving force. That, or a negotiated surrender, which would mean a further intolerable erosion of the centre, are the only ways out. And, within the traditional political

confines, there is only one source from which such a relieving force could
come: the power and money of the trade union leadership, increasingly
irritated by the intransigence of the Left. That would not be a healthy
form of relief. It would obviously and inevitably increase the political
power of the unions by making the Labour Party more and not less of a
trade union party. I do not think that would be good either for British
politics or for the unions themselves.

They already have great industrial power, and significant political
power as well. This is as much as they or any other estate of the realm can,
or should, carry. The unions have an essential and difficult job to do.
Sometimes they are too much criticised for the way in which they perform
an almost impossible task. But the idea that the British people want a
trade union dominated and nominated government on top of the power
the unions today exercise at the workplace is far from the truth. I doubt if
it would be elected, and if it were the unions would find it impossible to
discharge the schizophrenic role bestowed upon them.

What has all this to do with our sluggish economic performance? Our
great failure, now for decades past, has been lack of adaptability.
Sometimes this rigidity is a source of strength. It was very good not to be
too adaptable in 1940. But overall it is a source of weakness. Some
societies — France in the second half of the Third Republic, pre-
revolutionary Russia, the Austro-Hungarian Empire — have been still
less adaptable than our own. But they hardly provide grounds for
comfort. Compared with post-war Germany, post-war Japan, Fifth
Republican France (industrially at least), the United States for virtually
the whole of its history, compared for that matter with early Victorian
Britain — modern Britain has been sluggish, uninventive and resistant to
voluntary change, not merely economically but socially and politically as
well. We cannot successfully survive unless we can make our society more
adaptable; and an unadaptable political system works heavily against
this. Politicians cannot cling defensively to their present somewhat
ossified party and political system while convincingly advocating the
acceptance of change everywhere else in industry and society.
'Everybody change but us' is never a good slogan.

The paradox is that we need more change accompanied by more
stability of direction. It is a paradox but not a contradiction. Too often
we have superficial and quickly reversed political change without much
purpose or underlying effect. This is not the only paradox. We need the
innovating stimulus of the free market economy without either the
unacceptable brutality of its untrammelled distribution of rewards or its
indifference to unemployment. This is by no means an impossible
combination. It works well in a number of countries. It means that you
accept the broad line of division between the public and the private

sectors and do not constantly threaten those in the private sector with nationalisation or expropriation.

You encourage them without too much interference to create as much wealth as possible, but use the wealth so created both to give a return for enterprise and to spread the benefits throughout society in a way that avoids the disfigurement of poverty, gives a full priority to public education and health services, and encourages co-operation and not conflict in industry and throughout society. You use taxation for this purpose, but not just to lop off rewards. The state must know its place, which should be an important but far from an omnipotent one. You recognise that there are certain major economic objectives, well beyond merely regulatory ones like the control of the money supply, which can only be achieved by public action, often on an international scale. Two clear contemporary examples are first the breaking of the link, now fairly long-standing, but by no means inevitable, between economic growth and the consumption of oil; and second, by co-ordinated government purchasing policy, ensuring that this country and Europe as a whole is a major producer and not merely a passive purchaser of the products of the electronic/telecommunications revolution. Success or failure on these two points will largely determine whether we with our partners are a leading or second-rate industrial group in the world of the 1990s. You use market forces to help achieve such objectives but do not for a moment pretend that they, unguided and unaided, can do the whole job.

You also make sure that the state knows its place, not only in relation to the economy, but in relation to the citizen. You are in favour of the right of dissent and the liberty of private conduct. You are against unnecessary centralisation and bureaucracy. You want to devolve decision-making wherever you sensibly can. You want parents in the school system, patients in the health service, residents in the neighbourhood, customers in both nationalised and private industry, to have as much say as possible. You want the nation to be self-confident and outward-looking, rather than insular, xenophobic and suspicious. You want the class system to fade without being replaced either by an aggressive and intolerant proletarianism or by the dominance of the brash and selfish values of a 'get rich quick' society. You want the nation, without eschewing necessary controversy, to achieve a renewed sense of cohesion and common purpose.

These are some of the objectives which I believe could be assisted by a strengthening of the radical centre. I believe that such a development could bring into political commitment the energies of many people of talent and goodwill who, although perhaps active in many other voluntary ways, are at present alienated from the business of government, whether national or local, by the sterility and formalism of much of the political game. I am sure this would improve our politics. I think the results might also help to improve our national performance. But of that I cannot be certain. I am against too much dogmatism here. We have had more than enough of it. But at least we could escape from the pessimism of Yeats's 'Second Coming', where

> *The best lack all conviction, while the worst*
> *Are full of passionate intensity*

and

> *Things fall apart; the centre cannot hold.*

An Experimental Plane

The following months saw much media and other speculation about a new Party emerging. Within days of the Dimbleby Lecture Bill Rodgers, speaking at a Labour Party dinner in Abertillery, gave the clearest possible signal; he said that Labour had just one year to put its house in order.

Much to-ing and fro-ing between London and Brussels ensued. There were discussions, meetings, action and activity amongst the nascent Social Democrats.

In May 1980 there was a private meeting for members from all over the country of the Campaign for Labour Victory (CLV), a Centre-Right grouping of the Labour Party led by the so called 'Gang of Three': Bill Rodgers, Shirley Williams and David Owen. Bill Rodgers pointed out that only six months were left of his Abertillery ultimatum and Shirley Williams made it clear that Social Democrats within the Labour Party would no longer continue to 'provide a fig-leaf for the extremists'.

Within the Labour Party other leaders were obsessed with the question of the leadership succession to James Callaghan. Under the new Wembley rules the Trade Unions would play the major role. Many of their followers within the Parliamentary Party were, at that time, taken up with personal problems of re-selection. This led to a paralysis of will within the old establishment of the Labour Party. They were unable or unwilling to counter-attack against the great advances of the Left.

Since the Dimbleby Lecture political correspondents had moved from derision at the concept of a new political party and mass defections from Labour towards a growing awareness that this just might happen. Above all, the political community was waiting for Roy Jenkins to speak again: to clarify, to elaborate and perhaps to state his intentions. There was a silence for about seven months after his lecture until his next speech in England on 9 June 1980. Then addressing the Parliamentary Press Gallery, he spoke of launching an experimental plane.

This speech has suffered from a surfeit of anticipation. Whilst the fashionable political commentator's position is to be very cynical about the prospect of any political re-alignment — more so I believe than is the public outside politics and outside in particular the sometimes over-heated and over-crowded atmosphere of the Palace of Westminster —no-one could complain that cynicism leads to a lack of journalistic interest in the subject.

Roy Jenkins then outlined his personal plans. He would be staying in Europe as President of the EEC until the New Year of 1981, but no longer.

Does this have any political significance? I don't know. I expect nothing from British politics. They have been very kind to me in the past, and when I walked out of the House of Commons in December 1976, I assumed that I was doing so for the last time as a Member. I am not searching restlessly and demandingly for a rôle or a job, but I do reckon that the scene is sufficiently dismal to call for some comment at the present time, and that anyone who has spent half a life-time in the House of Commons and a decade as a Minister is not disqualified from making it; nor, for that matter, is anyone else!

In that spirit I gave the Dimbleby Lecture last autumn. I think that nearly all the thoughts I then expressed have since been strengthened. I was struck by the response which it evoked, not so much from the press or politicians, who were politely interested but for the most part sceptical and cool, but from the wider public. The letters I received, almost entirely from people I did not know, and mostly from people unknown to the national public but in many cases in positions of local but non-political influence, were striking, even more for their quality than for their quantity. I must not exaggerate. I have received more letters before — say when I resigned the deputy leadership of the Labour Party —although the postal charges were cheaper then! But I have never received before a great batch of mail which was first, ninety-nine per cent friendly; second, ninety-nine per cent sane; and third revealed, often argued over 400 or 500 words, such a degree of desire for release from present political restraints and for involvement in the future. I subsequently formed the view that as a basis for discussion of re-alignment it is inadequate to see British politics as two and a half bottles, one labelled Conservative, the next Labour, the third Liberal, and then to think in the fixed quantities of exactly how much you could pour out of each of the first two bottles and put alongside the third. We must think much more in terms of untapped and unlabelled quantities —and when you look at the low level of participation today — even the Conservative Government, with its big majority polled only thirty-three per cent of the electorate, the previous

Labour one only twenty-eight per cent — there is no reason to doubt that they exist.

I also devoted much of the lecture to arguing for proportional representation, the case for which is in equity overwhelming and the case against which has progressively crumbled. Proportional representation is not however a prior condition of a political re-alignment of the radical centre. A breakthrough, as opinion poll figures have shown, could be achieved without it, and a breakthrough should be used to make sure that proportional representation follows — it is apparently desired by nearly four-fifths of the electorate — and underpins the change.

I also spoke of the incompatibilities within the Labour Party, saying that some dispute and tension within parties was inevitable and indeed desirable but that when internecine warfare became the major and constant purpose of a party's life, when incompatible people and incompatible philosophies became locked in 'a loveless, constantly bickering and debilitating marriage', that was another matter. There were then and still are three major issues of constitutional dispute within the party, and I indicated why their importance was not so much inherent — in a cohesive party the outcome would not greatly matter. It is precisely because the party is a now incompatible marriage that it matters so greatly who chooses the leader, who writes the manifesto, who controls MPs.

But these constitutional arrangements are perhaps less important than the question of what the policies are, and what the party is committed to if it wins an election. Here again, almost without a struggle, we have just witnessed a major lurch to the left in policy making. The supreme authority of the Labour Party committed itself nine days ago to four policies:

First, a near neutralist and unilateralist position, which would make meaningless our continued membership of NATO and give us no basis on which to play an effective rôle in practical negotiation for arms limitation. And this within five months of the invasion of Afghanistan.

Second, a commitment to practical non-co-operation with the European Community leading in all likelihood to a firm proposal for complete withdrawal in the near future, in other words the total reversal within five years of the carefully built and democratically endorsed long-term direction of our economic and foreign policy. What flicker of reputation for consistency of purpose would we keep? What friends of influence would we retain? What loneliness do we seek?

Third, a massive further extension of the public sector, despite the manifold unsolved problems which beset our nationalised industries, and mounting evidence from all over the world that full-scale state ownership is more successful in producing tyranny than in producing goods. Capitalism has its crisis today, but so too does state socialism. There is now no economic philosopher's stone. But the more successful nations are those which embrace a mixed economy and follow it with some consistency of purpose, not forever changing the frontiers.

Fourth, what remains of the private sector is to have enterprise squeezed out of it by being subjected to a strait-jacket far tighter than in any other democratic country in the world.

This is not by any stretch of the imagination a social democratic programme. Nor do I believe that it is the way to protect Britain's security, help the peace of the world, revitalise our economy, or represent the views of the great majority of moderate left voters. Yet with a derisory 6,000 against (i.e. six real votes) it is what the Labour Party has committed itself to in the interests of party peace. And this was a party conference to which we are asked to give still greater powers for the future. And did it even win party peace?

There was no amity at Wembley and there has been no amity since. Once again great tracts of ground have been given up but not even an armistice, let alone a lasting peace, has been secured.

I therefore believe that the politics of the left and centre of this country are frozen in an out-of-date mould which is bad for the political and economic health of Britain and increasingly inhibiting for those who live within the mould.

Can it be broken? It is easy to say no. Mr. Callaghan, to whose firmness as Prime Minister and on incomes policy today I pay tribute, dismissed any new alignment last Monday in the following terms:

'Well, they will not get very far because any party in this country has got to rest on organised interests. We may or may not like that. The Tory Party rests on the support of big business, very largely business generally. It rests on the financial support of them and of the City. The Labour Party rests on the support of the trade unions and organised workers, and I do not think any other party is going to get very far unless it has some equivalent organised support and I do not know where you find it from'.

Very compelling *Realpolitik*. What do I say to that? What I say is this. Are you satisfied with that sort of politics based on industrial confrontation? Do you think it corresponds to the social structure of Britain today, as opposed to that of thirty or fifty years ago? And do you really believe that class politics, apart from being contrary to what a great part of the electorate wants, can set the framework for the co-operation in industry which is essential if Britain is not to continue straight down the road which leads to an industrial desert? It is a very conservative and very static view of politics. It is one which hands over to the Tory party the whole business interest and those who sensibly believe they have an interest in the success of British private industry. It hands them over to a far greater extent than I would be willing to do. And it is one which leaves the Labour Party far too dependent upon trade union support and control. To those who are satisfied with the present political map of Britain, who discount the manifold signs of growing alienation from the system and growing 'dismay' at its economic results, I have little to say. I do not doubt the strength of political inertia. I do not doubt the difficulty in this as in other fields of endeavour of doing anything new. The likelihood before the start of most adventures is that of failure. The experimental plane may well finish up a few fields from the end of the run-way. If that is so, the voluntary occupants will have only inflicted bruises or worse upon themselves. But the reverse could occur and the experimental plane soar in the sky. If that is so, it could go further and more quickly than few now imagine, for it would carry with it great and now untapped reserves of political energy and commitment.

There was once a book more famous for its title than for its contents called *The Strange Death of Liberal England*. That death caught people rather unawares. Do not discount the possibility that in a few years' time someone may be able to write at least equally convincingly of the strange and rapid revival of Liberal and Social Democratic Britain.

CHAPTER II

The Break Out

The Declaration for Social Democracy

Roy Jenkins's term as President of the EEC came to an end on 6 January 1981 and he returned to Britain. The Labour Party, in its agonies, occupied the centre of the stage in British politics. The October 1980 Labour Party Conference had consolidated left-wing policy and organisational triumphs, but the date of 24 January 1981 had a particular significance. This was to be the date of a special conference of the Labour Party, again to be held at Wembley, on the method of choosing the Leader of the Labour Party in Parliament. The man chosen would automatically become Labour's candidate for Prime Minister.

In the dying months of 1980, it became clear that the Left had triumphed. Through their union and constituency strength they had destroyed the Parliamentary Labour Party as a major force within the Labour movement. Re-selection of all sitting MPs between general elections created a new concept of temporary tenure. The only effective opposition being offered to these developments was from the 'Gang of Three': David Owen, Shirley Williams and Bill Rodgers, and thirty or so MPs openly describing themselves as Social Democrats loosely associated with the Campaign for Labour Victory. Already, this group had been dubbed 'exitists' within the Labour Party and with some justice. Enough lines had been drawn and Rubicons crossed to make a split almost inevitable.

The Wembley Conference took place on Saturday 24 January and completed the rout of the Parliamentary Labour Party. Their main prerogative had been to select the Leader. Now they had a thirty per cent say in that decision, while the Constituency parties had thirty per cent and, at forty per cent, the Trade Unions had the largest vote.

The miracle which alone could have averted the split in the Labour Party had failed to materialise. On Sunday 25 January 1981, the day after the Wembley Conference, the Gang of Three and Roy Jenkins, eighteen days after his return from Brussels, assembled at David Owen's house at Limehouse.

What now became known as the 'Gang of Four' jointly contributed to, and issued, what was heralded as the Declaration for Social Democracy.

The Declaration for Social Democracy

The calamitous outcome of the Labour Party Wembley Conference demands a new start in British politics. A handful of trade union leaders can now dictate the choice of a future Prime Minister. The Conference disaster is the culmination of a long process by which the Labour Party has moved steadily away from its roots in the people of this country and its commitment to Parliamentary government.

We propose to set up a Council for Social Democracy. Our intention is to rally all those who are committed to the values, principles and policies of social democracy. We seek to reverse Britain's economic decline. We want to create an open, classless and more equal society, one which rejects ugly prejudices based upon sex, race or religion.

A first list of those who have agreed to support the Council will be announced at an early date. Some of them have been actively and continuously engaged in Labour politics. A few were so engaged in the past, but have ceased to be so recently. Others have been mainly active in spheres outside party politics. We do not believe the fight for the ideals we share and for the recovery of our country should be limited only to politicians. It will need the support of men and women in all parts of our society.

The Council will represent a coming together of several streams: politicians who recognise that the drift towards extremism in the Labour Party is not compatible with the democratic traditions of the Party they joined and those from outside politics who believe that the country cannot be saved without changing the sterile and rigid framework into which the British political system has increasingly fallen in the last two decades.

We do not believe in the politics of an inert centre merely representing the lowest common denominator between two extremes. We want more, not less, radical change in our society, but with a greater stability of direction.

Our economy needs a healthy public sector and a healthy private sector without frequent frontier changes. We want to eliminate poverty and promote greater equality without stifling enterprise or imposing bureaucracy from the centre. We need the innovating strength of a competitive economy with a fair distribution of rewards. We favour competitive public enterprise, co-operative ventures and profit sharing.

There must be more decentralisation of decision making in industry and government, together with an effective and practical system of democracy at work. The quality of our public and community services must be improved and they must be made more responsive to people's needs. We do not accept that mass unemployment is inevitable. A number of countries, mainly those with social democratic governments, have managed to combine high employment with low inflation.

Britain needs to recover its self-confidence and be outward looking, rather than isolationist, xenophobic or neutralist. We want Britain to play a full and constructive role within the framework of the European Community, NATO, the United Nations and the Commonwealth. It is only within such a multilateral framework that we can hope to negotiate international agreements covering arms control and disarmament and to grapple effectively with the poverty of the Third World.

We recognise that for those people who have given much of their lives to the Labour Party, the choice that lies ahead will be deeply painful. But we believe that the need for a realignment of British politics must now be faced.

SHIRLEY WILLIAMS   ROY JENKINS   WILLIAM RODGERS   DAVID OWEN

25 January 1981

The Social Democratic Party

On Thursday 26 March 1981, after two months of turmoil and of almost monopolising British political news, the Council for Social Democracy became a fully fledged political party.

At a press conference held in London at the Connaught Rooms in Covent Garden, the four leaders each made two-minute statements to the world's political press. This was Roy Jenkins's contribution.

It is exactly two months since we launched the Council for Social Democracy. Today it becomes the Social Democratic Party. It is the biggest break in the pattern of British politics for sixty years — two generations.

But we are not just offering another player in the old party game.

We are saying that the rules of the game itself, with its unfair electoral system, big minorities almost unrepresented in the House of Commons, people feeling they have to choose between two rigid party machines neither of which they like very much, violent swings of policy based on small shifts of opinions, have damaged British industry, destroyed British jobs and undermined the prosperity and influence of this country.

We offer not so much a new party — although it is that — as a new approach to politics. We want to get away from the politics of outdated dogmatism and the politics of class confrontation. We want to release the energies of people who are fed up with the old slanging match. There is a lot to be said for the enterprise of the individual, but the individual cannot live on his own, without caring for those around him.

We believe that in friendly arrangements with the Liberals we can achieve a major breakthrough by the next general election. We believe we can reconcile the nation and give Britain a renewed purpose and success.

C H A P T E R   I I I

The Making of the Alliance

A Partnership of Principle

The new Social Democrats understood two critical facts about their chances of electoral success. First, that to fight the two great parties that had for so long alternated in government, would demand all of their resources and that to take on the Liberals, in addition, would be suicidal. Second, that the Liberals already occupied a sizeable part of the terrain in which the SDP needed to become established.

It was a matter of great good fortune that there were no differences between the terms of the Declaration of Social Democracy and Liberal Party policy so fundamental as to constitute an unbridgeable gap between the two parties.

Meetings between Labour Party 'exitists' and senior Liberals, particularly between their leader, David Steel, and Roy Jenkins became more frequent as the option of defeating the Left in the Labour party receded. During the two-month interval between the Limehouse declaration and the Connaught Rooms press conference, these contacts increased at every level as groups of Social Democrats began to emerge throughout the country.

With some understandable apprehension, Liberals started to respond to the break-up of the Labour Party and the emergence of a new political force that seemed to stand for much that the Liberals had held dear during their long years as a minority party.

Five days after the launch of the SDP, Roy Jenkins held out the hand of friendship to the Liberals. On 3 March he spoke to the Gladstone Club at a National Liberal Club dinner.

There are many issues which divide Mrs Thatcher and Mr Michael Foot. But two emotions unite them. The first is a deep fear that the two-party monopoly of British political power, secure for fifty years, is about to be cracked. The second is a sustaining hope that the monopoly could still be saved by dispute between the Liberals and the Social Democrats. Our determination must be to underpin the fear and undermine the hope.

If we fail to work together in a partnership of mutual respect and trust we shall throw away an opportunity which will not come again in this generation. You could preserve your ancient purity and we could enjoy our exciting novelty, but the old monopoly would survive, unloved, uncreative, but almost unscarred, and both of us, and more important, Britain, would be the losers.

There is no reason why we cannot honourably and constructively collaborate. We have different traditions, although yours is one which, partly because of my amateur historical writings, I think I understand and certainly respect. But that difference of tradition can be a source of strength rather than of weakness. It can give us together a wider appeal, and as our aim is to reconcile the nation and transcend false and out-dated divisions of class and dogma, that is a great advantage.

If we turn from the past to the present we have no differences on the major issues facing the country. I am sometimes asked accusingly 'What are the disputes between you and the Liberals?' Answers do not readily come to my lips, although I — and you — could no doubt find some, if we searched hard. But why should that closeness of view be a matter of reproach? If we were proposing an arrangement purely of convenience, even of opposites, a new version of a Fox-North coalition, that would seem to me rather discreditable, and would be seen as such by many people. How much better that we should be able to envisage a partnership of principle: agreed upon the main issues; affronted, as is so much informed opinion from the leading economists to the Confede-ration of British Industry (CBI), by the lasting and unnecessary damage being inflicted upon our economy by the present Government; positive in our support for the mixed economy; resolved on electoral reform; determined on maintaining Britain's international links.

We need neither exaggerate nor be ashamed of our distinct identities. Together we can change the shape of British politics and revitalise the country. In sterile dispute we can damage each other while achieving little for either of us. If anyone chooses that route they will bear a heavy responsibility for having thrown away a remarkable opportunity.

The Llandudno Speech

Within nine weeks of the launch, Roy Jenkins was precipitated into the Warrington by-election, where he stood as the Social Democratic Party candidate with Liberal support.

It was a major characteristic of this campaign that large numbers of election workers, both Social Democrats and Liberals, arrived, worked together in a wholly integrated way and rejoiced together at the dramatic result (see page 52).

On 15 September 1981 Roy Jenkins and Shirley Williams were enthusiastically welcomed by a fringe meeting of the Liberal Assembly in

Llandudno. Roy Jenkins opened his speech by referring to a trail-blazing event of the year before.

Only twelve months have passed since David Marquand spoke with David Steel at a meeting similar to this one. But that year has opened the greatest prospect of change in British politics than any we have seen for sixty years. The issue before us is whether we, Liberals and Social Democrats, so conduct ourselves between now and the next General Election that the prospect becomes a reality: a reality which breaks the stultifying monopoly of power which the two big parties have for too long enjoyed; a reality which means full-scale electoral reform at the earliest possible moment so that that unfair and damaging monopoly cannot remain; a reality which frees the electorate from the false choice between the equally unwelcome extremes of Mrs Thatcher and Mr Benn; a reality which offers a new and widely sought-after hope to the British people.

Three questions pose themselves. First, is the Alliance necessary? Every shred of evidence confirms that it is overwhelmingly so. Separate we might remain interesting, although I expect that you would find that if we were to pull apart, the present mood of pulsating political excitement would be quickly dissipated. But together we are formidable.

Second, will it work? I do not doubt that there will be problems and that they must be settled on the ground. But on the ground it can, must, and, most important, does work. It worked at Warrington. The Liberal support that we received there was quite simply magnificent. I believe there was hardly a Liberal who did not enjoy working with the Social Democrats, and hardly a Social Democrat who did not enjoy working with the Liberals.

Third, is the Alliance creditable? Is it honest? Again I answer unswervingly 'yes'. We are sometimes accusingly asked where we differ. Some differences do of course exist, but they are mainly those of tradition, or provenance. They can actually add strength to the Alliance. For our objective is to achieve a wider goal and to transcend outdated divisions of class and dogma. There are a few of policy, but they are incomparably less than those which divide Mrs Thatcher and Mr Prior, Mr Healey and Mr Benn.

We are united . . . we can therefore honourably achieve not a marriage of convenience but a partnership of principle. I would go further and say that it can be still more. To use an old Gladstonian phrase, it can be a union of hearts. We can of course let all this slip. You can fall back on your ancient purity and we can console ourselves with our exciting novelty. But what fools we would be if we did! Mrs Thatcher and Mr Foot would heave sighs of relief. Still more important, a great part of

public opinion would experience a sense of disappointment and let-
down. The monopoly would survive unloved, uncreative and almost
unscarred. This will not happen. We have jointly made an unprecedented
opportunity. Let us seize it together in an alliance of mutual respect and
mutual trust.

The Perth Meeting

*Following the September Assembly of the Liberals in Llandudno, the
SDP held its first members' national meeting in Perth on 4 October
1981. Roy Jenkins was able to give rather more than a progress report.*

This party is still less than seven months old. Its impact and its
achievement during the 192 days since that wet and hazardous morning
of the launch on 26 March has been greater than our highest hopes. We
have confounded the sceptics. We have enthused our followers. We have
rallied our Liberal allies. We have touched a chord in the British people
which has brought them to public meetings, up and down the country,
from Guildford to Glasgow, from Taunton to Leeds, on a scale not seen
for a generation or more. We have pricked the bloated bladders of
complacency which for so long cocooned the two big monopoly parties.
How complacent they were! 'Dead as a dodo, mere fluff', Mr Callaghan
said of the idea of us, under a year ago. 'Absolute bunk' had been Mr
Healey's contribution a few months previously. Mrs Thatcher at least
described what she called 'the new Limehouse Left' as a slow poison. We
have established a new style which has brought back politics from the
professionals to the people. We have astonished the world.

We have created the greatest opportunity for change for sixty years.
Yet let us be clear how much we still have to do, that it is still only an
opportunity, and not an accomplished, underpinned reality. We must
ourselves beware of the complacency which we rightly mock in others.

We have probably two years, possibly less, perhaps as long as two and
a half, between now and the General Election. On that our main sights
must be fixed, although there will be many important engagements on
the way; Croydon, into which we must put at least as much Social
Democratic effort as the magnificent support which the Liberals gave us
at Warrington; Crosby, other by-elections, local by-elections, in which
we have achieved so many notable victories; and then the main local test
next spring.

Roy Jenkins went on to review the results of two-and-a-half years of doctrinaire rule and incompetent monetarism. He described the Labour Party as unable to offer a constructive alternative. He then set out the basis of the new politics, defined the tenets of Social Democracy and spoke of relations with the Liberals.

We are far more than a reaction to events in the Labour Party. We have a momentum of our own. We bring with us the best part of the old non-dogmatic Labour spirit of conscience and reform, the tradition of the party of Attlee and Gaitskell. But we have also drawn together many of other political affiliations and of none. We welcome former Conservatives who believe in one nation but not in one narrow and misguided nostrum. We welcome former Scottish Nationalists, whose commitment to Scotland marches alongside our own commitment to decentralisation, who want decisions taken closer to the people but who reject the destructive extremism and lack of respect for the rule of law which is at present sweeping through that party. We welcome too those of public spirit but no previous party commitment, whose political energy has been dammed up by the sterility of the old politics.

We are open to all who accept the basic tenets of social democracy. These tenets are simple and direct as have been all the mind-shifting messages of political history. But they are neither soggy, nor all things to all men. They are unacceptable, certainly in whole and mostly in particular, to the leadership and militants of both the monopoly parties. They comprise:

First, a commitment to a fairer electoral system which will give proper representation to all major strands of opinion; provide a less violently alternating and therefore more efficient framework of government; and help to avoid the political polarization of the nation into north and south, industrial and rural, city and suburban.

Second, an industrial policy which will end the futile frontier war between public and private sector, which will pay equal respect to both service to the community and to the initiative, enterprise and profit-making which are essential to the vigorous functioning of a market economy, which, while it cannot do everything, is better at producing more of the goods that people want than any centralised system that has ever been invented. But we insist equally that a sizeable part of the wealth so created must be used to correct social injustice, heal the wounds in our cities, and protect our environment.

Third, a repudiation of the excessive centralisation and the pursuit of bigness for bigness' sake which, under governments of both parties, has made both politics and industry too remote from the people.

Fourth, a belief in a Britain that is tolerant at home, absolute in its commitment to racial equality and the rights of the individual, and self-confident, internationalist, dependable, and involved abroad. This means that we accept the full commitments of membership of NATO, that we are not going to turn round like squirrels in a cage on Europe, and that we see no moral or economic security for a rich West which attempts to ignore the poverty of the Third World.

All those who share these principles are welcome in the SDP. But it is no place for class warriors, for those who want to fight the sterile, doctrinaire battles of yesteryear, for little Englanders, for racial bigots, or for those whose narrow self-interest makes them indifferent to the society and the world around them. We demand no rigid orthodoxy from our members. Free men and women do not all think alike on every issue. What we do expect, and have so far overwhelmingly found, is a degree of common approach and mutual goodwill which will enable us to discuss issues and construct policies without the atmosphere of bitterness and internecine warfare which breeds bludgeons in the Labour Party, and daggers — mostly in the back — in the Conservative Party.

We believe that this common approach and mutual goodwill can and must extend to our relations with the Liberal Party. With them we have what is at once an alliance of interest and a partnership of principle. At Llandudno it was triumphantly underpinned and came near to being a union of hearts as well. Let us do nothing to tear it apart for, make no mistake, it is not possible for Social Democrats to break the stultifying grip of the two oligarchical parties and battle with the Liberals as well. It is unnecessary and to let it happen would be an act of frivolous, self-indulgent folly on both our parts. It would rejoice the symbiotic hearts of Mrs Thatcher and Mr Foot and it would both disappoint and disillusion millions of people throughout the country. They want and need the Alliance. And the polls show it.

There is no point in office for the sake of office. There is great point in office to change and improve Britain; to break out from the sterile conflicts of class and dogma which have bedevilled both politics and industry; to begin with electoral reform, an overdue process of constitutional change, at once liberating and stabilizing, such as we have not had for nearly a century; to bring the nation together and to replace fear with hope in the hearts of the people; to introduce a new politics which can be more relevant, more representative, closer to the people; to give Britain an opportunity to recover its industrial strength at home and its self-confidence and influence abroad.

The Liberal Assembly, Bournemouth

Nearly a year later, on 25 September 1982, Roy Jenkins once again addressed a Liberal audience. This time it was the Liberal Assembly at Bournemouth. There had been triumphs and vicissitudes for the parties of the Alliance — the Croydon triumph of Liberal William Pitt; Shirley Williams back in the House of Commons after a stunning SDP victory at Crosby. But 1982 started badly for the Alliance with a temporary breakdown of good relations over the decisions as to which party should fight which constituency. This coincided with a concerted push by Tory proprietors and editors of Fleet Street newspapers to halt the runaway successes of the Alliance by minimising coverage of its activities. Great pressure was also put on the BBC and ITV companies to curb the extent of vital television exposure.

The opinion polls had, at times, predicted an overall parliamentary majority for the Alliance but did so no longer. Roy Jenkins himself re-entered the electoral fray, contesting and winning the former Tory seat of Glasgow, Hillhead in a by-election. The Alliance recovered momentum and Mrs Thatcher got the lowest poll ratings of any Prime Minister since polls began.

It was in this context that the Falklands war took place. A small war, a long way from home, but one which gripped the interest of the British people for three months. While the drama was being played out, everybody felt involved. Domestic politics were put on the back burner and the political phenomenon of the Alliance was squeezed out of the news. With the military victory in the South Atlantic, the fortunes of Mrs Thatcher and the Tory Government recovered and were once more in the ascendant.

Throughout the late summer, units of the Army, Navy and Air Force returned home to a heroes' welcome. The opinion polls now showed that Mrs Thatcher was the most popular Prime Minister since Churchill. It was clear that she would claim the spoils of victory by calling an early general election.

This was the political scene as the 1982 autumn Party Conference season began. Roy Jenkins's task, like that of all the Opposition leaders, was to try to turn the interest of the electorate back to the domestic failures of the Conservative Government in what was likely to be the run-up to a general election.

I believe I am the first leader of a British party ever to address the Assembly or Conference of another.

A year ago at Llandudno we spontaneously turned the Alliance, which had previously existed only tentatively and informally, into a partnership of principle. And we swept forward from there to the great autumn victories of Croydon and Crosby. I do not believe for a moment that either could have been achieved without the Alliance.

Meanwhile we began the hard process of allocation of seats. In fact, this has almost throughout gone remarkably well, given the inherent difficulty of the job. To bring together an old party of tradition and a new party of bounding novelty, as we certainly were in 1981, and to decide that in half the constituencies each had to divert from the main purpose of political action, was bound to be a formidable task. It is easy to understand how in a local context some on either side cannot see why they should give way. Yet in a national context the need has always been overwhelmingly clear. We are not avaricious heirs dividing up pieces of property of a fixed value, so that any accommodation leaves one side worse off. Our aim is to win seats, not just to fight them. And in unity and amity we can win more than in altercation.

All the evidence is that we suffer peculiarly from bickering and disunity. There are very good reasons why this should be so. One of our strongest joint appeals is first that we offer an escape from the 'what we have, we hold' approach of the politicians of the two old monopoly parties; and second that we can bring the nation together and transcend the damaging bitterness of out-of-date class-based politics. Both these points are valid. But they will not seem valid if we quarrel over spoils before they have even been won, or if we cannot even bring ourselves together.

The fact of the matter is that the agreements have always outnumbered the disagreements; but it is the disagreements which get the publicity. There has been a great deal of self-sacrifice within both the Liberal Party and the SDP. A most notable example of the former was at Hillhead where, with the seat looking easier to win at that stage than it subsequently turned out to be, your candidate, Chick Brodie, stood down because he believed it to be in the interest of the Alliance. And he worked at my side throughout the campaign, which did indeed greatly underpin the unity of the Alliance in Scotland. He was there on the platform when Jo Grimond confessed that though he had been sceptical in 1980 and 1981, he now saw his dream of the early 1960s becoming a reality. The idea of re-alignment in politics stemmed from him more than from anyone else. David Steel and I are lucky enough to have the opportunity of turning into reality the idea of which Jo Grimond dreamt over half a generation ago. But if we now let the opportunity slip it will be much more than half a generation before it comes again.

We are both of us — and many others too — determined not to let it slip. That means that we must now regard the argument about seats as finally over, that we must accept that we both have a fair deal, and make it stick.

Having settled our own affairs we must turn outwards to the public. Both in the SDP and in the Alliance we have been too internally occupied for most of 1982. Now we must speak to the nation, not further negotiate with each other, and we must speak a message of both hope and realism, such as is coming from neither of the complacent parties. Let us talk sense to the British people.

The immorality of the Government's position is that they build hopes of winning the next election on spreading fatalistic hopelessness about any reduction in unemployment below the present three-and-a-half million. What a recipe for a dangerously split society! What an abandonment of hope! Nothing like it has been heard since the chorus of self-satisfied obeisance to market dogmatism which came from President Hoover and his cabinet before they were swept from power in 1932.

But at least the Hoover administration, although inflicting great poverty on the richest nation in the world, was not destroying the long-term basis of American industry. But that is exactly what the Thatcher government is doing here. They are not only robbing people of jobs today. By allowing much of British industry to die under their eyes they are killing the prospect of jobs in the future.

The Labour Party has hope but no sense. It persists in its belief, against all the evidence, that a further massive dose of unwanted nationalisation, plus centralised planning of everything except incomes, plus a protectionism which would cut us off from sixty per-cent of our export markets, which would be pharisaical towards the Third World and invite retaliation from the developed world, is the answer to our problems. I have not the slightest doubt that Mr Foot would like to get rid of unemployment. It is not about that that he and the Labour Party, unlike Mrs Thatcher, are complacent. It is about believing in the old dogmatic discredited measures of isolationist state socialism plus a special contracting out pass for trade union power that they are complacent. This recipe will not work. I have equally little doubt that the Labour programme with its mixture of improvident finance, quitting the EEC, and threatening every successful business within sight, would worsen the state of the economy and not make it better. Unemployment would be higher, not lower.

What are the lessons of France in the past year? Mrs Thatcher thinks they prove the case for petrified inactivity. Mr Foot just tries to ignore them. I believe that experience is relevant and that what we should learn from it is this: in a poor world climate, if you want to expand the economy, for God's sake do not undermine the confidence of private business at the same time.

Most jobs must come from the private sector. But they will not come unless the Government provides some stimulus. But the stimulus will not work unless the private sector has the confidence to respond. This is where the contribution of the Alliance can be unique.

What do our two parties jointly offer? First, by electoral reform, on which we are totally agreed, we can provide a more stable framework of government, within which industry can operate and plan. The threat of minorities using temporary command of the House of Commons to impose irreversible changes would be removed.

Second, a truce in that endless debilitating battle over the frontier between the public and private sectors, which has done as much damage to British industry in the past thirty-five years as the battles for Alsace-Lorraine did to European peace and prosperity over the previous eighty years. We are agreed to that.

Third, the need, now greater than ever, to instil a new spirit of partnership in industry. Nothing has done this country more harm than the 'us against them' view, rather than a mutual commitment to the success of the enterprise, whether private or public. And our adversarial, class-based politics have spilled over into industry and encouraged precisely this warring and destructive spirit. We need a major drive for profit-sharing, workers' co-operative schemes, democracy at the work place if we are to begin to overcome this. We are, I believe, agreed about that.

Fourth, we need not weaker trade unions but more democratic and responsive ones. Just as through electoral reform we want to restore politics to the people, so through secret postal ballots for election of general secretaries and executives we want to restore the unions to their members. We are, I believe, agreed about that.

Fifth, we want initiative and enterprise to create wealth, and we want success to be rewarded fairly, even generously. But we also believe in policies of social concern, of caring for the weakest. We are implacably opposed to any mad Thatcher/Tebbit bicycle rides back before Attlee, back before Beveridge, back before Lloyd George, to a poor law concept of the health service or other social provision. It is not only Labour extremism but Tory extremism which threatens the sense and stability of this country. I hope and believe that the Tory wets will at last revolt at such a determined attempt to re-create two nations. Whatever they do, we shall be implacably opposed to such atavism. We are agreed on that, I believe.

Sixth, we must never forget that we are, both of us, firmly internationalist parties. Two parties led by the members for Roxburgh and Selkirk, and Glasgow, Hillhead have no room for little Englanders. But we have no room for little Scotlanders or little Britain-ers either. This is not because we believe in bigness for its own sake. We want decisions to be taken increasingly at as intimate a level as possible. The most foolish view is that the gentleman in Whitehall should always decide. Quite often it is better done in Glasgow or Edinburgh (or Berwick-on-Tweed, or Truro, or Ely).

But sometimes also it has to be done, if it is to make sense, in collaboration with Brussels, or Washington or New York. A rigid fixation on decision making at the national level can be wrong both ways round. That is why we must stay in Europe, strive to prevent nuclear war not pretend we could contract out of it, and reject the view that there is either sense or morality in turning our backs on the grinding poverty of two thirds of the world. We are agreed on that, I believe.

Our areas of agreement are vast. Our islands of disagreement are tiny. Just as there is an unhealthy hypocrisy in politicians who fundamentally disagree clinging together on the raft of a bankrupt old party because of the coldness of the sea around them, so there would be an equal hypocrisy in politicians who agree as much as we do, Liberals and Social Democrats, pretending that we must keep apart and stress our differences. That would be to let down millions of people in the country, people who want a new deal in British politics and who believe that only a Social Democratic/Liberal Alliance can provide it. When we have hesitated over our Alliance, so they have hesitated over their commitment. The time for hesitation is passed. Let us go forward together to make a reality in 1983 of the great prospect which we opened up in 1981.

The First Alliance Meeting

At Westminster Hall on 20 January 1983 the first major Alliance rally took place. With Mrs Thatcher's prestige running high in the wake of the Falklands victory, 1983 was to be Election year.

The Westminster Hall rally included the many hundreds of Liberal and SDP prospective Parliamentary candidates who had been selected to fight constituencies. As was appropriate to such an occasion, there were speeches from all the major leaders of both parties. It seemed, when Roy Jenkins spoke, it was as the commanding general addressing his troops.

April, as Eliot wrote, may be the cruellest month. But January is the most challenging one. Three years ago today I was not quite sure where we would go after the Dimbleby Lecture, and the commentators were almost unanimous in saying nowhere. Two years ago today we were on the brink of the Limehouse Declaration, but it was still far from certain that we would issue it, and still less certain that it would lead on, in two months' time, to the birth of the first major British political party for eighty years. A year ago today we were at the beginning of the ten-week Hillhead campaign, perhaps the longest and most fluctuating by-election campaign recently fought.

Fluctuating fortune and snatching victory out of the jaws of defeat has therefore been the life-style of the Social Democratic Party, and of the Alliance, of which we are proud to be a part. We were born to live dangerously. We have destroyed safe seats for others and cracked the cosy framework of two-party politics. By the same token we cannot expect safe seats or easy victory for ourselves. But we have great opportunities. Looking at the varying prognoses of the past three years, I reject utterly the defeatist view that our correct strategy is to go for a balancing bridgehead in the next Parliament. Everything is to play for. Total victory is perfectly possible. And this, and nothing less, is our objective.

There is today a compelling and spectacular need for a new radical reforming government. The rhythm of history calls for one. There has been an extraordinary regularity about the emergence of such governments, extending back over 150 years and with deep roots in Liberal history. In 1830 the Grey Government, which carried the first Reform Bill, came in. Thirty-eight years later there was the first Gladstone administration, which set a new pattern of politics for two generations. Thirty-eight years after that we had the great 1906 Liberal victory, and everything which flowed from it: the 'People's Budget', the crushing of the absolute powers of the House of Lords, and the foundation of the Welfare State. Thirty-nine years later we came to 1945, the best ever Labour Government, when Beveridge was made reality by Attlee and Bevan, when full employment was first achieved in peacetime, when Ernest Bevin's response to the Marshall plan set Europe upon its feet again, when we saw what could be done by imaginative international co-operation, and when the Western world began the greatest advance to prosperity ever seen in recorded history. Thirty-eight years from then takes us to 1983.

Thirty-nine years, of course, takes us to 1984. If it were a Labour victory, I think it would be uncomfortably close to George Orwell's 1984. We would cut ourselves off from most of the Western world. We would be out of Europe without even the democratic courtesy of a second referendum. With sixty per cent* of our export market thus imperilled, there can be no doubt that we would plunge into the most narrow-sighted protectionism. This would be destructive for us, still proportionately the most export-dependent major economy of the lot. It might also be decisive for the world trading system. This system is evenly balanced for

---

* Fifty-nine per cent to be wholly accurate, the proportion of our exports then going to the rest of the European Community and the countries around it with which the EEC has free trade arrangements.

the first time for a generation between, on the one hand, the liberal trade regime which has served so well the prosperity of nations and, on the other, a plunge back into the cut-throat economics of the twenties and thirties. The irony is that a British unilateralist lead on disarmament, to which Mr Foot is so attached, would almost certainly be followed by no-one else, but that a protectionist retreat could well have a major repercussive effect. The Labour policy would not lead the world to safety, but it might well lead it to impoverishment.

It would certainly make a mockery of our membership of NATO. It would certainly lead to a massive further dose of unwanted, irrelevant and damaging nationalisation. Its attitude to education and to health care would run us straight up against the European Court of Human Rights. And the more they found against us, the harder such a government would dig into the bunker.

Ah, you may say, but nice Mr Foot, and Mr Healey and Mr Shore do not really believe in all that. Do not be taken in. They are committed to the policies, which are now not even argued about in the Labour Party, and they are only sustained against the depredations of the hard left by the uncertain, undemocratic and constitutionally undesirable support of a handful of trade union leaders. The constituency parties, as they become still more narrow caucuses, go ever more to the left. Eighty per cent of them voted for Mr. Benn. And they choose the MPs of the future. So, of the three bases of power in the Labour Party, one, the constituency parties, has already gone. The second, the parliamentary party, is as a result going. The third, the union hierarchy, is a matter of chance, and ought in any case not to be in the game of making Prime Ministers and imposing policies.

Can Mr Foot be a bastion against that? Hardly, on the basis of his performance over Mr Peter Tatchell. What a debacle for him the last fortnight has been! Never, while he was leader, he proclaimed, would Mr Tatchell be a Labour candidate. A faint whiff of grapeshot from Bermondsey was all that was necessary to destroy that heroic stand. And what did Mr Foot end up by doing? He *seconded* Mr Tatchell's endorsement. He might at least have proposed it, or opposed it, or abstained. But to *second* it was surely the ultimate humiliation. So put not your faith in the old guard Labour leadership! A Labour victory would not be a return to relevant radicalism. It would be much more of an approach to 1984 in the Orwellian sense.

Our sights are firmly on 1983, be it June, be it October, be it any month. And we intend that to be the beginning, not merely of a new government, but of a new period of politics, innovative, libertarian, close to the people, but above all based on reconciliation, rather than digging deeper and deeper into the divide of politics.

D

Let there be no doubt that such a divide is what this Government offers. This is why not merely the dates but the circumstances call for an Alliance victory. To accept three-and-a-half million unemployed, and to hope to win an election upon their backs, is in itself an immoral acceptance of a split society. There is no other major country with unemployment as high as in Britain today. Yet there is no other, either, in which it is accepted so complacently by the Government of the day. Japan successfully contains the problem. Germany, with a bigger population, shudders at two million. France, of which Mrs Thatcher was so contemptuous when it did two more or less planned devaluations, taking the currency down by effectively fourteen per cent may actually have made some progress and got back to 1.9 million. Having produced her own totally unplanned collapse of last week, when market forces — which she had previously patted on the head like junior and suitably dry members of her Cabinet — suddenly behaved in an independent and displeasing way, the Prime Minister might perhaps be a little less complacent. But I doubt it. She is cocooned in self-righteousness. She still proclaims that she has made British industry more competitive, while in fact she has destroyed much of it. She is then surprised and complaining that people buy so many imports. To have reduced manufacturing output to its 1965 level is a remarkable feat by any standard.

The Prime Minister further divides the nation by adopting a stance on nuclear weapons which makes her the best recruiting sergeant for the unilateralists. She is in danger of being left in a far more rigid position than either most leaders of American opinion or the other European governments.

Let us not underestimate the wide current of concern about the nuclear threat which runs through the country. It is in no way confined to unilateralists, still less to those who want Russia to be strong and the West to be weak.

There are millions of people who do not believe that unilateralism would either provide for the proper defence of the country or help world peace, but who nonetheless believe that there is now a real opportunity to reverse the unnecessary and dangerous build-up of mutual terror. But all that they get from the Prime Minister is a slavish repetition of the slogans that President Reagan is preparing to abandon. Zero option cannot be both the beginning and the end of the negotiation. That would mean no negotiation.

Let us never forget that we are both of us, Social Democrats and Liberals, firmly internationalist parties. That is why we do not deceive ourselves that we can contract out of nuclear danger. If nuclear war occurs it will not just be those who live around a base, or even in a particular country, who will be at risk. It will be the whole of civilisation. All our efforts must therefore be devoted to preventing such a catastrophe. And that demands vigorous action to make the progress which is now possible in both sets of Geneva talks.

Our internationalism also means that we see Britain's economic problem in a world context. We can do a good deal here at home. We can reverse the trend and prevent Britain's unemployment being the worst in the world. We have set out our detailed, practical, carefully costed programme for creating over a million jobs in eighteen months to two years. That demands action from the Government and a confident investment response from private industry. The Tories will not provide the action. Labour would kill the response.

But we also need urgently to help stop the whole world from spiralling down still deeper into what is already the worst slump for fifty years. 1983 offers a real opportunity of change of direction. An Alliance government would say three things to our major trading partners. First, let us make a concerted, practical plan to expand together. It is more secure and sustainable that way. Second, let us get some sense into the international monetary system. We should get into the European Monetary System and inside it help to form a tripod of stability between the European Currency Unit (ECU), the dollar and the yen. Third, there must be greater flows of finance to the poor world. Otherwise markets will collapse still further and we shall all be dragged down. This is not soft-hearted generosity. It is enlightened self-interest, and good common sense.

I believe that the mood of the world is now ripe for such a major initiative. But there is no leadership. All it gets from the Government — Prime Minister and Chancellor — is lectures in favour of further restriction and a repetitious and totally misplaced complacency about the future. We would provide such leadership. We would provide a message of hope for the world which would have a direct impact on jobs here at home.

But the Alliance is not just about economics. It sprang out of a revolt against the sterility and divisiveness of our out-of-date, out-of-joint political system. Everything, from the House of Commons to the electoral system, is based upon confrontation. And that confrontation preserves class, entrenches dogma and divides the British people. Moreover it infects the whole industrial climate and creates the biggest drag upon Britain's chances of sustained recovery.

In every field, education, democracy in industry, the social services, Parliament, the voting system, we offer radicalism in the cause of reconciliation. We are for change, but change that will last, and will bring together the nation. Our appeal is broadly based across the regions and nations of Britain, across the classes, across the occupations, across both sides of industry. We in the Alliance are working together in a partnership of indissoluble principle. We are working together for Britain. We offer our fellow citizens the opportunity to work together in the same way, for the regeneration of our country.

CHAPTER IV

The Personal Campaign

Warrington: the Acceptance Speech

Barely sixty days after the launching of the SDP, it was announced that the Labour MP for the safe seat of Warrington had been made a judge. A by-election would have to be held.

That an election test for the fledgling party should come so quickly was a trick of fate of a kind for which British politics is famous. That it should fall in one of Labour's safest constituencies was particularly unlucky.

Given that Warrington was an unpromising constituency, there were many senior figures in the SDP who thought that the prestige of the new party should not take the risk of Roy Jenkins standing. Perhaps a worthy local candidate could be found or one of the less nationally prominent ex-MPs might be prepared to fight?

Through this cloud of indecision and perhaps on the principle of 'put up or shut up', Roy Jenkins offered himself to the local SDP, was enthusiastically adopted on 11 June 1981, and threw down the gauntlet to the established parties.

It is with a sense of deep commitment that I accept your invitation to be Social Democratic candidate for Warrington and to fight the first parliamentary election on behalf of the new party. My commitment is both to the people of Warrington and to the purposes of the SDP, which can and will change the landscape of British politics.

The two are not separate. The primary concern in Warrington is employment, not merely amongst the 8,100 in the travel-to-work area without work, but amongst others who fear the future. There is nothing in this respect for which to thank the last Labour Government, let alone the present Conservative Government. The Labour Government produced an increase of unemployment of over fifty per cent in five years. The Conservative Government has produced an increase of 160 per cent in two years. Industry, which is the major source of jobs here, as in so many other constituencies particularly in the North and Midlands, has suffered far too long from being the shuttlecock of old-style dogmatic politics.

Each government has come more and more to reverse the economic policies of the previous one. Nationalised industries and the private sector alike have been threatened by one side or the other, and have seen no consistent framework within which to plan for the future. Pointless changes of ownership, nationalisation, de-nationalisation, re-nationalisation, have greatly exacerbated the problems of the steel industry, for example, which would in any event have been great. The two old monopoly parties have fought like quarrelsome ambulance men over the sick body of this industry, on which many others depend, while neglecting its real problems of structure, investment, productivity and jobs. The result is plain to see. And its effects have spread far beyond one industry.

We have a dangerously low level of investment, first in the public sector, owing to government restriction, which fails to make the necessary discrimination between current and capital expenditure and has allowed the proportion of capital expenditure to fall within the total from twenty per cent to eight per cent over the past ten years; and in the private sector, where lack of confidence and low profitability under a Conservative Government's severe recession and threats for the future from a left-wing Labour Party combine to produce an atmosphere of apprehensive caution instead of one of buoyant hope.

The result has been slump in the capital goods and construction industries with a declining general level of international competitiveness made worse by a foolish policy of indifference to the exchange level of the pound.

The effect of politics in our traditional adversarial, in and out, blame-the-other-side-for-everything style, has given our industry one of the least stable frameworks of almost any industrialised country in the world within which to plan and develop the future.

The effect has been made worse by violent switches not only every four or five years when governments change, but every two or three when they reverse their own policies and try to undo some of the damage that their own baggage train has inflicted on the country in their first years of office. This happened in 1972, it happened also in 1976, and, who knows, it may not be far off now.

The industrial results lie around us. They are to be seen in our shrinking industrial base, our mounting unemployment, our disused factories, the irreversible disappearance of many previously successful export lines.

This has been brought to a head by two years of doctrinaire and incompetent monetarism. I am not against an adequate control over the money supply. I am not against discriminating stringency in public expenditure. I practised them both in the late sixties, but combined with unemployment below 600,000 and inflation not much above five per cent.

I am against the unthinking stubbornness which refuses to recognise the near impossibility of getting public borrowing down in conditions of deep recession. The costs of unemployment and high interest rates on state expenditure, the loss of state revenue from low profits and two-and-a-half million without earned incomes, are too high for that. To try to push on through that blocked route is like getting a car stuck in the mud, and getting in still further by spinning the wheels round faster. This Government offers little hope. It has already done great damage with perverse side effects. It has increased the proportion of public expenditure in the national income. It has increased the total weight of taxation. It has not only weakened the community services and nationalised industries. It has also weakened much of private industry. It is a failure.

But the Labour Party of today, with its out-of-date, inward-looking restrictionist policies offers no constructive alternative for the future of our industry and the jobs which depend upon that. It would snuff out such remaining confidence as exists in private industry. Its narrow protectionism would invite retaliation against our exports, leaving us all worse off at the end of the day, would further reduce our competitiveness and would starve us of valuable inward investment, whether from Europe, America or Japan. It would be a recipe not for prosperity and security but for a big move towards a Polish-like economy.

Yet there is not the slightest reason for despair. If only we could get a government which would stop doing a lot of foolish things and do instead a few wise ones which would stick, spare us from unnecessary and queasy rides on the ideological big dipper, treat public and private industry with equal respect, encourage long-term planning and profitable investment in the former, and initiative and risk-taking in the latter, we could begin to turn the tide.

There is an alternative. There is an approach which will substitute hope and confidence for gloom and new despair, which will enable us to turn our backs upon our nagging fear.

I do not pretend that we can at all quickly get back to what were previously regarded as tolerable unemployment levels. It will be a long and difficult struggle. But we could begin to escape from the ridiculous position in which, in a world still reeling from the blow of the 1979 second oil price surge, we, who because of the North Sea ought to be the most immunised against this, have produced the deepest recession of the lot.

Immediately we should move to a position in which, instead of frittering away our oil reserves, we use the period of relative ease with these reserves to mount a major programme of renewing our badly out of date public infrastructure: railways, public transport generally, the expansion of British Telecom, water and sewerage systems, as well as energy saving and insulation work and the development of renewed sources of energy.

This in itself would give a big stimulus to the private sector, where well-judged investment should not be dictated but encouraged to be more profitable by interest rate and other measures. Vocational training for the young and re-training for those further on in life should be strongly and urgently developed.

The effect on a town like Warrington, with its excellent communications and wide spread of industries, including within the area many with a high technology base, could be dramatic. It is not always possible for people to remain in the same jobs, but nor need they stagnate in a climate of constant job decline.

This by-election shows every sign of putting Warrington on the political map. I hope that the widespread attention it will generate will also help to give it an economic shot in the arm.

All this, however, demands not merely a change of economic policy but a break-out from the confines of the existing political system which has been ossified for far too long. It has not merely been a particular government or a particular party which has recently failed us, but the system itself.

First, its winner-takes-all, first-past-the-post system has come to encourage extremism, which is against the mood of the majority of the British people. It enables a very limited number of militants by controlling the machine, the label and the loyalty which they hope goes with it, to hold many moderate people within the party prisoners, because they think their seats and any influence depend upon retaining the old label. I think they are wrong, but that is what they believe.

As a result the Labour Party has moved from being a party of fraternity to being a party of fear. Everybody fears some other group, but most of all they fear Mr Benn. They feared to elect Mr Healey leader, Mr Foot feared to challenge the Wembley Conference. But now, driven beyond endurance, seeing one after another of good loyal members refused reselection, on grounds not of their performance but of their honest views, Mr Healey, Mr Shore and Mr Hattersley are saying even worse things about the Labour Party than we were a few months ago. If you thought we were exaggerating, listen to them.

But it is already too late. The pass has been sold. The slide has become irreversible. Who would have thought a few years ago that first Mr Foot would have become leader, and that then, within six months of his election, he would be being bitterly attacked for being too *right*-wing a leader?

Second, the system has become more manifestly unfair. Thirty years ago it under-represented, and that not by much, only three per cent of the voters. Now it grossly under-represents a growing twenty five per cent. Meanwhile the old arguments for the present system become increasingly threadbare. It does not produce strong, consistent, coherent government. It does not avoid incompatible coalitions; no coalition could be more incompatible than the present Labour Party. If it formed one, its next Cabinet would be a shambles of warring groups. A far more compatible coalition would be formed between the Social Democrats and the Liberals. Electoral reform — proportional representation — is urgently necessary on grounds both of fairness and of coherent, steady government. It would be one of our highest priorities.

Third, the present system, with its sterility and the artificiality of the political slanging match, has repelled many people of energy and public spirit, who often play a large part in voluntary organisations, from active participation in either national or local politics. We want to bring them in — or, in some cases, back in — and the nature of our response shows that we are being remarkably successful.

Our sights as a party are very high. We want to show a way out from the old debilitating politics of out-dated dogmatism, remoteness from the thoughts of ordinary people and encouragement of false class confrontation which have bedevilled this country.

In partnership with the Liberals we believe that we can form the next government of this country. This by-election is a key stage on that journey. It is not, of course, on its history and voting pattern an easy seat for us. If we could win it, we would be likely not merely to achieve government, but to sweep the country with an almost unprecedented majority. That sort of result does not fall off trees.

It will, as from tonight, be a difficult struggle, but we will face that struggle with the utmost determination and vigour. We will seek in the course of it to underpin our partnership with the Liberals. We will give a clear Social Democratic message to the people of Warrington, and through them to the nation. We will engage with both Warrington and national problems.

I cannot of course claim to be a local candidate. It was not possible to have both that and one of the founders of the party. But the idea that I have served my political life in rolling pastures or leafy suburban avenues, which some newspapers seem to suggest, is ludicrous. I have represented one of the most industrial seats in Birmingham for twenty-seven years and I believe I had happy relations with them. I certainly won nine elections there.

I will devote myself to Warrington interests and a Warrington campaign. We shall not fail for want of resolve and commitment. Together we can wage a great, even a memorable fight. I thank you warmly for your confidence.

From Warrington to Hillhead

The SDP and Alliance campaign gathered momentum and took off. By fielding the architect of the new politics, it ensured that, whatever else happened, the world's political press would be there, speculating about whether the new party might, as senior Labour politicians hoped and forecast, be effectively snuffed out in this one by-election.

SDP workers poured in to help. More than half of the members were new to party politics. Their enthusiasm compensated for their inexperience.

Seasoned Liberals, particularly from their nearby redoubt in Liverpool, were there in large numbers and experienced 'exitists' from the Labour Party managed the campaign with flair and skill.

To the 'exitists' there was a cleansing, purgative quality in the campaign. At a later date, Roy Jenkins described it as follows:

> *'I know of no-one who has come out of the Labour Party into the SDP who begins to cast a backwards glance of regret. On the contrary, we feel liberated and re-invigorated. As was much noted by those who came to Warrington, we enjoy our politics for the first time in years. We speak unmuzzled and we carry our heads high . . .'*

Enjoying politics was certainly a common experience for the Alliance workers when the result was announced. It was reported by The Times *on 17 July 1981.*

ROY JENKINS SLASHES LABOUR MAJORITY: TORY LOSES HIS DEPOSIT
by Julian Haviland and Philip Webster

Mr Roy Jenkins and the Social Democrats, in their first public test sixteen weeks after the formation of their new party, yesterday jolted both the Government and the Labour Party by taking two out of every five votes cast in the Warrington by-election.

The triumphant former deputy leader of the Labour Party claimed at once that it was the most sensational result of any by-election for decades. It would imprint itself on the country's history, he said.

Labour's Mr Douglas Hoyle, the left-wing former MP and member of the party's National Executive Committee, came out on top. But a rock solid Labour stronghold, held by 10,274 votes at the last election (a majority of 32.6 per cent) is now a marginal held by 1,759 (or six per cent).

The Conservative, Mr Stan Sorrell, the London bus driver who is an office-holder in Mrs Margaret Thatcher's constituency party and a personal friend of hers, was beaten out of sight, his deposit lost with those of the eight other minor candidates.

The Conservatives were no-hopers from the first, but so contemptuous a dismissal by the voters of Warrington is something the Government would like to have been spared.

He has one crumb of comfort. There is little doubt that some Conservatives deserted him for Mr Jenkins, whom they saw as the likeliest candidate to give Mr Hoyle and the Labour Party a stinging rebuff.

The SDP's decision to fight the Warrington by-election, which fell in the wrong place for them and before they were ready, had been triumphantly justified.

Their morale is now high. Their credibility has been established. Their ability to organise and to tap new sources of political commitment, particularly among young people, has been demonstrated impressively.

Only about seventy seats in Britain, most Labour held, are safer than Warrington. The challenge for the SDP was not only that Labour was deeply entrenched, but that there was no traditional third party vote to build on.

The Liberal candidate in Warrington took only nine per cent of the vote at the general election of 1979, when the average Liberal vote in the English constituencies was 14.5 per cent. So the potential support in English seats, for an alliance between Liberals and Social Democrats must be some five or six percentage points higher than the SDP's share of yesterday's poll.

In parliamentary terms, this means that a repetition across the land of yesterday's astonishing result would put an SDP/Liberal government in power at Westminster with a crushing overall majority.

That is fantasy, of course. At a general election the Alliance would not have scores of Roy Jenkinses, nor enough helpers to make their Warrington effort on a front 600 times as wide.

But it is the kind of fantasy that may summon up infinite new energy among many who ponder the Warrington result.

Yet every allowance must be made for the freakishness of by-elections, and their proven tendency to exaggerate a political mood.

If the SDP need sobering today, they may reflect on the Chester-le-Street by-election, in March, 1973, when the Heath government was unpopular.

The third party then, the Liberals, secured 38.6 per cent of the vote from a standing start, having had no candidate there at the general election three years earlier.

But they were beaten in the general election the following year, and only fourteen Liberal members were returned to the Commons.

Mr Jenkins said that it was the most sensational result of any by-election in recent decades. It far exceeded the SDP's highest expectations.

Mr Jenkins, his voice full of emotion, said the figures, translated on the national scene, meant there was a prospect of a Social Democratic—Liberal government at the next election with an overwhelming majority.

He said it was the first Parliamentary election he had lost but 'it is by far the greatest victory in which I have ever participated'.

'I congratulate Mr Hoyle on achieving the lowest Labour vote in this constituency — the lowest percentage in this constituency — for fifty years'.

Mr. Hoyle, visibly shaken by the result, claimed that he had secured a magnificent victory against a press campaign that had never before been seen in recent political history.

Mr Hoyle branded the SDP as a 'media created party' which would fade from the political scene as quickly as they had risen. 'There is nothing to unite this party', he said.

Jenkins took 42.4 per cent of the poll, and Hoyle 48.4 per cent. This was a swing to the SDP (Lib) of 23.3 per cent. The Tory share was 7.1 per cent.

Mr David Steel, the Liberal leader, said it was an outstanding result. The lessson was clear for members of his party — there could be no turning back. 'We go on now with the formation of an alliance which will form the next government'.

He said that this was not a by-election swing against the Government. The Government was flattened. It was a swing against the official Opposition at a time of government unpopularity.

Mr Steel remarked: 'There is no good news in this for Mrs Thatcher. There is no good news in this for Michael Foot. There is tremendous good news for all those people out in the country who longed to change the political system.

'The monopoly of power that the Tory and Labour parties have held since 1924 has been busted in Warrington. Warrington has spoken for England and, I suspect, it has spoken for Scotland, Wales and Northern Ireland tonight.'

Mr Alan Beith, the Liberal Chief Whip, said Roy Jenkins had been an outstanding candidate but the result could not have been achieved without an alliance. Together they could produce a Liberal—SDP government after the next election. 'If we do not work together we cannot achieve that. After this we will be more determined than ever to work together.'

Mr Michael Foot, the Labour Party leader, described the results as a crushing vote of no confidence in the Government.

Lord Thorneycroft, the Conservative Party Chairman, said: 'I congratulate Mr Roy Jenkins on dealing a dramatic blow to the Labour Party in what was regarded as a safe Labour seat'.

Mr Stanley Sorrell, the Conservative who lost his deposit, said it had been a tactical vote to keep out an ultra left-winger. He was sad that it had failed because Mr Hoyle had no mandate from the people of Warrington.

'We have lost a battle but we have not lost the war', he said.

Warrington established the SDP as a serious political force and Roy Jenkins emerged with enhanced personal stature, with many regarding him then as the uncrowned Leader of the SDP.

1981 brought the formalising of the Alliance with the Liberal Party and the first by-election success for the new force. The Liberal candidate, Bill Pitt, who had come fourth in the Croydon constituency only two years previously, now won the seat. In October the Conservative seat of Crosby fell vacant on the death of its MP. He had been returned with a majority of 19,272 in 1979.

A Liberal candidate, Anthony Hill, who had fought the General Election, was already in place. He displayed great generosity, particularly in the light of his Liberal colleague's success in Croydon. He stood down to make way for Shirley Williams. Her brilliant victory saw out the historic year of 1981.

These by-election victories brought external dividends to the Alliance but created internal tensions between the two parties. Constituencies, previously hopeless, began to look winnable and so the competition for them quickened. By January 1982 some of the shine had disappeared from the brand new Alliance. This coincided with a sea change in the approach of newspapers, radio and television as Tories and Labour alike exerted all their influence to stop the publicising of the Alliance parties and personalities.

It was against this background and its consequential loss of support from the polls, that Roy Jenkins was adopted as SDP Liberal Alliance candidate for Glasgow, Hillhead on 14 January 1982. A by-election had been called because of the death of the Conservative incumbent.

Hillhead: the Acceptance Speech

There was a Liberal candidate in place, Chick Brodie, but he stood down, also with great generosity, to make way for so experienced a statesman. Here again, in Roy Jenkins, the Alliance put one of its most valuable assets at risk. As 'The Times' commented later: 'A magnificent failure like that at Warrington might have damaged him beyond repair, even if he could have found the spirit and the opportunity to try again'.

This, the fourth by-election since the Alliance was founded, was the first in Scotland, a factor heavily emphasised by Roy Jenkins in his acceptance speech. He gave particular attention to the thorny problem of devolution.

Britain, and in Britain perhaps above all the West of Scotland, needs a change of shape of politics such as only the Alliance can provide. I am not a Scotsman. I am not a Glaswegian. I have a Glasgow degree, but proud though I am of it, that hardly counts. But what I believe I do have is a profound sense — and that not recently acquired — of the remarkable history of this city, particularly over the past 130 years. Britain could never have achieved its full greatness without the self-confident contribution of Glasgow. That greatness, assisted in the process by the increasingly sterile dogmatism of the two old parties, has flowed away from Britain. And no city has suffered worse from the efflux than has Glasgow, which a century ago brought so much to the rising tide of prosperity.

It is never sensible to try to set, in exactly its old form, the past upon its throne again. But what is needed, and is possible, is the recovery in new forms of the innovating self-confidence of the West of Scotland. I believe that Glasgow needs a powerful new voice in the councils of Westminster and of Whitehall. I would be proud to try to help provide it.

The central issue of the by-election is the reversal of the industrial decline of this city and region. This shows itself most obviously in the unemployment figures. But it goes still further than that and affects the whole framework of civilised life within which the immensely difficult social problems of a contracting city have to be handled.

The Alliance can make a unique contribution. We reject the class-based politics on which the two adversarial parties have flourished. It is an outdated approach no longer in accordance with the desires of the majority of the people. And while the monopoly parties may have flourished upon this diet, little else has. Such a political approach has inevitably encouraged confrontation in industry, and that has had a particularly damaging effect upon the prospects of this city and region of

Scotland. We stand for an approach which reaches across the classes to bring people together and not to tear them apart.

Social Democrats also stand for bringing politics and power back to the people. I said in the Dimbleby Lecture over two years ago, when the new party was just a gleam in my eye, that I wanted to devolve decision making wherever we sensibly could. We fully recognise the special needs and identity of Scotland. I set out my views on that issue on an occasion when, whatever else I was doing, I was not seeking votes, in Scotland or elsewhere. It was on 26 March 1976 at Inverclyde. I had just withdrawn from the second ballot for the leadership of the Labour Party, and had already been offered the presidency of the European Commission.

My views then were and are now that I believe in the integrity of the United Kingdom, but I also believe that this is more likely to be fortified by a well worked out system of devolution than by a rigid attachment to excessive centralisation. And if this devolution can come as part of a general constitutional reform, involving acceptable and economical decentralisation for England as well, so much the better. This must not involve excessive delay. But the Scottish scheme must be built to last, which means that it must command widespread cross-party support and not be cobbled illogically together to serve short-term electoral purposes. That was a large part of the trouble last time.

Done in this way it should also bring a new feeling of self-reliance to Scotland, which would help with the central economic problem. But that also demands that industry and the economy as a whole must cease to be the shuttlecock of old-fashioned doctrinaire politics from which they have too long suffered.

Immediately we should stop frittering away our oil revenues and start to use the limited period of relative ease which these revenues bring to mount a major programme of renewing our badly out-of-date public infrastructure.

This in itself would give a big stimulus to the private sector . . .

The effect on the Clyde region, with its skills and wide spread of industries, including many now with a high technology base, could be dramatic.

His political prescription followed, encapsulating the developed philosophy of the Alliance parties.

The fight is on. We cannot yet tell exactly when the election will be. Whenever it is, we shall be ready for it. We will wage a memorable Hillhead campaign, and I believe secure a famous victory. I will serve the constituency to the utmost of my ability. I would be proud to be a member for Glasgow.

Our keynote must be the restoration of confidence. We must show that there is an alternative. There is an approach which will substitute hope for fear. A hundred years ago this month Franklin Roosevelt was born. Fifty-one years later he started to give a depressed America a new deal, a new confidence, a new freedom from fear. He did it without doctrinaire ideological baggage, without out-of-date class dogma, but with a determination to make things work better and to give his great nation an opportunity to escape from its head down attitude and restore its verve and its greatness. We need a touch of that in the heart of Scotland and in Britain as a whole today. Let us try to infuse this campaign with such a message of unifying hope.

Hillhead: the Victory Speech

At 1 a.m. on 26 March 1982 Roy Jenkins, after an absence of five years, was returned as a Member of Parliament with a majority of 2,038 votes over the Conservative, Labour's candidate coming third and the Scottish Nationalist fourth. He was understandably cheerful speaking at the count.

This result is a great satisfaction to the SDP and Liberal Parties in the Alliance.

The election has not been without its ups and downs . . . marked by the close and reflective interest of the electorate. The outcome is a triumph for the new deal of sense, moderation and hope which we have offered to the people of Glasgow. The result matches our highest expectations.

Hillhead has rejected the Conservatives for the first time since 1918. The Labour Party continues to maintain its record of not gaining a by-election since 1971. The Alliance has polled well in every part of the varied constituency, thus under-pinning our claim to represent all sections of the community in Scotland, as in other parts of the UK.

This is a magnificent first birthday present for the Social Democratic Party.

The Press reports were even more euphoric.

The Guardian:
Mr Roy Jenkins and the Social Democratic Party are back in the running today as a major force in British politics after a spectacular victory in the Hillhead by-election. Both the Conservatives and the Labour Party suffered a heavy humiliation.

For Mr Jenkins, it was a matter of rather more than political satisfaction. Victory now makes him an almost certain leader of the SDP and a probable leader of his party's alliance with the Liberals. Defeat could have relegated him to political retirement.

Financial Times:

Mr Roy Jenkins returned to the centre stage of British Politics early this morning. He won the Glasgow Hillhead by-election by 2,038 votes after one of the most dramatic and closely fought contests for decades.

His return to Parliament after his absence of five-and-a-half years makes him the favourite to become the leader of both the Social Democratic Party and the SDP/Liberal Alliance.

Mr Jenkins' victory will also revive the recently flagging political momentum of the Alliance ahead of the May local elections.

Mr Jenkins received 10,106 votes, 33.4 per cent of the total, taking the seat from the Conservatives who had held it for sixty-four years. He wiped out a Tory majority of 2,002 at the last general election.

Admitting that the campaign had been the toughest he had fought, Mr Jenkins said the result laid to rest the 'myth that the Alliance did not have policies.'

The other parties immediate response was disappointment, especially since Mr Jenkins's winning margin was larger than predicted by the polls.

Comparison with the Alliance's victories at Croydon and Crosby last autumn is complicated by the involvement of the Scottish Nationalists producing a four-party contest. While the result is not as spectacular as the earlier ones, it suggests that the Alliance has regained some of its earlier momentum to become a major force in the run-up to the next election.

Turnout was 76.3 per cent of those eligible to vote. This is very high for a by-election so nobody can blame abstentions for the outcome.

Mr Jenkins' tough battle has, however, shown that the Alliance still faces strongly entrenched loyalties, making any breakthrough more difficult than the SDP's founders hoped.

The by-election has been regarded by all parties as one of the most important since the war.

Defeat might have halted Mr Jenkins's career as a major political figure for the time being, caused a divisive leadership contest within the SDP and inflicted a major blow on the Alliance's hopes of breaking the mould at the next election.

For both Conservatives and Labour, Hillhead offered a crucial chance of robbing the Alliance of credibility. The outcome underlines the problem both parties face in rebuilding.

It was a famous victory. Make no mistake of that.

E

By capturing the Conservatives' last seat in Glasgow, Mr Roy Jenkins has not just re-written the political map. He has brought off a spectacular gamble.

The most incredible thing is that in Glasgow at a time of nearly three million unemployed, with the Government half-way through its term, Labour still couldn't win this marginal by-election.

There is so much polish, so much style and so much affectation too that it is easy to miss something else about the reborn Roy Jenkins — his sheer political recklessness.

When he wanted to tackle Hillhead, half his own party thought he had taken leave of his senses. Glasgow, they said would never take to his style. No poll suggested that it was clearly within his grasp. But Roy was willing to risk all.

Now he has won it, what does it mean?

For a start, it has proved that the Alliance can fight and win on any kind of political terrain.

The first result will be a revival in the national poll position of the SDP. The party has depended all along on a diet of sensation, a bandwagon effect. How quickly we had all forgotten that remarkable Crosby result back in November.

Perhaps the greatest effect of Mr Jenkins's win on his own party will be to teach the political virgins aboard that the party can ride through the troughs in public opinion and come up on the next wave.

The Times:
TRIUMPHANT JENKINS BOOSTS CLAIM TO SDP LEADERSHIP.

Mr Roy Jenkins won the Glasgow Hillhead by-election for the Social Democratic/Liberal Alliance last night, securing for the party he helped to found a year ago its most notable advance and for himself an irresistible claim to its leadership.

Three months later when the SDP leadership election took place, what may have looked irresistible in the immediate aftermath of Hillhead now looked a little less so.

The SDP Leadership Address

On Friday 15 April 1982, the Argentine military government landed a substantial body of troops to recover the Falkland Islands by force and thus settle the long-standing dispute as to their sovreignty.

The House of Commons called into session on a Saturday, 3 April, agreed with rare bi-partisan unanimity to despatch a powerful task force immediately to evict the interlopers and restore the British presence.

The miltary campaign dominated press and television coverage and overshadowed domestic political matters such as the fortunes of the Alliance and the election for the leadership of the SDP, due to take place in June 1982.

For Roy Jenkins, the leadership election meant another gruelling campaign — his third in twelve months. Although Warrington had established both the SDP and himself, and Hillhead had restored Alliance fortunes and seemingly confirmed his 'de facto' leadership, he was not to be allowed an uncontested victory.

Dr David Owen, one of the two members of the Gang of Four who were still in the House of Commons at the time of leaving the Labour Party, had decided to run for the leadership. He had been thrust into the public eye by the events in the South Atlantic.

Because of his special knowledge of the Falkland Islands and a record of success in that area when he had been Foreign Secretary, he became a much featured specialist on television and radio programmes as well as in the press. His knowledge of the subject and his crisp, clear interventions in the House of Commons had brought him to the attention of the public in general and to members of the SDP in particular.

The leadership election was not to be a walkover but a tough political contest requiring a thoroughgoing approach to the SDP members who were to vote by means of a postal ballot. Here is Roy Jenkins's election address.

This is the third 'election address' which I have written in the past year. On the two previous occasions the task was more straightforward. I then used all the compressed cogency I could command to shift votes to the Social Democratic Party, and thus at Warrington to put us on the electoral map, and at Hillhead to keep us there.

Now we are engaged in an election within the Party. Some want to see it as a contest between conflicting ideologies. I do not believe that. Differences of view occur within the leadership. But they do not follow any pre-ordained line-up. Still less do they fit a Left/Right pattern. It was in any event to get away from such sterile misleading labels that many of us broke out of the old politics. The SDP is the most spontaneously united grouping that I have seen in politics. No leadership contest must disrupt that natural and valuable harmony.

Throughout the seventies I came increasingly to feel that the times were out of joint for British politics, and that it was not one government or one party which was failing the nation, but the system itself. By November 1979, when I gave the Dimbleby Lecture, I had become convinced that these faults could not be cured without a new political party, offering an escape from the class and dogma-based politics of the old Conservative/Labour axis of power.

There was a ripple of response, for many were looking for something which could either re-kindle, or create in them for the first time, a sense of political commitment. But 1980 was a year of scepticism. Those still active in party politics were wrestling with their loyalties. The commentators were cynical. Contrary to some recent views, the birth of the idea of the SDP was not easy.

Then came the great breakthrough of Limehouse and the launch, then a slight sag, then the by-election successes, and now the mists of the Falkland Islands crisis. When they disappear, Britain's problems will not have been solved. Nor will the analysis of these problems, out of which the SDP sprang, have been invalidated. The need and opportunity will still be there.

There are two questions of direction. First, our relations with the Liberals. This is a vital alliance which has worked well on the ground. At its best it is a real partnership of principle. Our separate SDP identity is, however, essential to the whole enterprise. It is our creation which has lit a flame in the country. We can be firmly for the Alliance, while proud of our distinct SDP philosophy and membership, which many have worked so hard to create.

The second question is whether we aim primarily at Labour or Conservative seats and votes. It is our intention and desire to win some of both. Indeed we have already done so. It is the only way in which we can make the Alliance the government of the country. Nor, within the Alliance, is there any question of our fighting only the traditional Labour seats. We are proud of the classlessness of our appeal, and of the wide range of political and non-political backgrounds from which our members come. Nevertheless it is the Labour Party that we are most likely to drive out of the arena of government. Our historical role will almost certainly be to take over as the main political force opposed to the Conservatives.

We are a radical party and must remain one. But our radicalism does not spring from the need to seek a particular segment of votes. We are radical because the country is in desperate need of change: constitutionally, industrially, socially. We need change that will stick, not the largely irrelevant and too easily reversible changes of recent governments which have paradoxically left us an almost uniquely hidebound and unadaptive society.

Our message is one of sense and hope, but it is also one of hard practical challenge. On unemployment, on democracy in the voting system and in industry, on a constructive commitment to Europe, on our determination to attack poverty and prejudice at home and abroad, we are specific and innovative.

We are certainly not all things to all people. As our policies develop we alienate some. But do not let us underestimate our appeal. We have come an immense distance in a very short time. If we keep our nerve and our sense of direction we can make the breakthrough at the next crucial General Election.

Handing on the Leadership

On the Sunday before the SDP leadership election, the Observer *poll gave David Owen an eighteen per cent lead, but four days later, Roy Jenkins won by a significant margin amongst SDP members.*

The victory, but not the spoils.

The Gang of Four still functioned with Roy Jenkins primus inter pares. *Owen, with substantial personal support, remained part of the Gang of Four but he also occupied a position outside and separate to the Jenkins-Steel nexus.*

In the aftermath of the successful Falklands expedition, the Government chose June 1983 for the Election. They won with an increased majority.

After only two years of the Alliance, the SDP and Liberals together totalled twenty-six per cent of the poll, nearly overtaking Labour at twenty-eight per cent. However, for 7.75 million votes for the Alliance against Labour's 8 million, only twenty-three seats were won compared with Labour's 209.

Two out of the Gang of Four, Roy Jenkins and David Owen, held their seats. But the overwhelming fact was that Mrs Thatcher's Government, although gaining fewer votes than at the previous election, had now an overall majority of 140, ensuring a four or five year period in office.

On 13 June, a Monday only four days after the election and at a time when the press was full of speculation about the fate of Michael Foot, leader of the badly beaten Labour Party, Roy Jenkins issued this statement after announcing his own resignation:

At the beginning of a Parliament which is clearly going to run for some years, I regard it as desirable that the SDP should immediately have a leader for the next election. Fortunately, with David Owen's victory at Devonport, such a leader is available.

It is for the SDP MPs to nominate and for the membership of the party as a whole to make the decision. But I hope that David Owen may be elected without a contest, and will lead the party to the full success that its solid basis in votes makes possible.

My handing over the leadership certainly marks no withdrawal from full political activities. I shall be particularly active in safeguarding the unity of the Alliance, in promoting the ever more necessary cause of electoral reform, and in representing the interests of my constituents in Hillhead.

The SDP Conference, 1983

A year after losing the SDP leadership election, David Owen became its leader. He immediately established himself, with only five SDP MPs behind him, with a dazzling and energetic display of leadership qualities. Roy Jenkins' supporters considered the 13 June statement to be a laying-on of hands, and thus the leadership changed hands with support from all sections of the Party.

Everybody realised that the next stage could be a long march with all the physical and psychological exhaustion this involved. David Owen had both the youth to take this on as well as the seniority for the leadership. There was also a suspicion that the next election would be fought like an American Presidential election, that is to say on the battlefield of television. David Owen excelled in television interviews and debates.

The experimental plane which Roy Jenkins had first talked about in June 1980 had proved its airworthiness. It was time, in the judgement of its designer and test pilot, to hand over the controls.

On Sunday 11 September at the 1983 Conference of the SDP at Salford, Roy Jenkins delivered his leader's valediction and confirmed the anointment of his successor. It was three years and ten months after the Dimbleby Lecture.

Since I last spoke to the Council at Newcastle in January, a lot has happened. We have fought a general election and secured a percentage of the vote which no new grouping in any stable democracy had ever previously attained. Of course the result even in terms of votes did not match our highest hopes. But 7¾ million votes for the Alliance, almost evenly shared between the two parties, was nonetheless a remarkable achievement and has been universally recognised as such. We have lessons to learn, but we certainly have no need of an inquest.

We have not done it all in one go, but we have come through a fierce test; and, if we play it right, we have a splendid prospect opening up before us. The days of anyone pretending that we are not a major long-term political force are decisively over. Mr Callaghan once described us as 'a bit of fluff'. That 'bit of fluff' has in the past few weeks been accepted by both Mrs Thatcher and Mr Kinnock as the principal menace to them — both of them.

That is excellent.

Of course in terms of seats the result was both a disappointment and a disgrace. It was a disgrace because of the distortions of the electoral system, which in a three-party situation makes our democracy a rigged lottery and not a rational system of representation.

It was a bitter disappointment not only because of the narrow misses, but also because of the loss of many outstanding parliamentary colleagues. They are lost, for the present, to the House of Commons. But they are not lost to Social Democracy. It is a tribute to the morale and conviction of the party that I know of no-one, however great the personal sacrifice, who regrets the deliberately hazardous step which he or she took in 1981.

Also, since I last spoke to the Council, I have passed on the leadership. It follows from what I have just said that I did so in no mood of defeat or dismay. I was proud of the campaign that we all fought. I feel a considerable sense of achievement in the distance that we have come since I launched the idea in the Dimbleby Lecture forty-six months ago. I regard the past two-and-a-half years, with its three personally fought election campaigns, and which have themselves been only incidents in one long continuing campaign and dialogue with the electorate, with only the geography occasionally changing, from Crosby to Gower to Peckham, with of course Warrington and Glasgow thrown in — I regard them as being one of the most testing but also best-spent periods of my life.

But I was also clear that the time had come for a change. It would not have been right for the newest party to have continued far into this Parliament with the oldest leader. And 'if it were done . . . then' twere well it were done quickly'. And when I look at what has been happening in some other parties this summer, I am more than ever convinced that I was right. We order these things better in the SDP.

The position was of course made much easier because David Owen, with his exceptional parliamentary talent and other outstanding qualities, was the obvious, available and natural choice.

I assumed and greatly welcomed his uncontested election. I congratulate David and wish him well. A large part of all our futures is now bound up in him.

I come to that future. First I must tell you that I in no way propose to contract out. My commitment will be complete. Second, I see one relatively easy task and another much more difficult one for us ahead. The first is decisively to replace the Labour Party as the effective opposition and alternative government. That means that a lot more former Labour voters must come over to us. Of course we want them. But we should not be a receptacle for despairing Labour politicians who fought against Alliance candidates at the last election. Genuine intellectual conversion, yes of course. But a careerist collapse into our arms, no.

The second and more difficult task is to accomplish this re-shaping of the political map without twenty years of Conservative hegemony — which is exactly what occurred the last time the political map was reshaped in the twenties and thirties. The disintegrating Labour Party we elbow aside. But it is Mrs Thatcher and her new model Conservatism that we have to beat. It can be done. This Government has immense weaknesses both of men and measures, as it was already showing in July.

But it will not be easy and will certainly require an effective, cohesive Alliance, which is attractive to the public because it is bound together not just by need but by the closest bonds of agreement and respect and warmth. Let us be in no doubt that the Alliance worked well during the election. It worked pretty well at the top, but above all it worked on the ground, where we enjoyed working together without demarcation, and where the close mingling in mutual effort soothed away most of the scars of seat allocation.

I do not fear that the Alliance will disintegrate. The ties of mutual interest are too close for that. What I do fear is a more subtle and insidious form of weakness. If on either side we allowed narrow party chauvinism to develop, we might become a little like the European Community at its worst: held together by material self-interest, but without a sufficient sense of common ideals and purpose to maintain a hold on the hearts of the people. That would be very damaging to our electoral momentum. It need not happen.

There is another consideration. No relationship in human affairs can remain static. This is true between individuals and between institutions. Either relations advance or they recede. We do not want recession. We must therefore be prepared for an advance and I believe a substantial advance.

In the SDP we must all be sensitive to each other's different susceptibilities. There is no point in splitting the SDP in order to unite the

Alliance. Nor would I wish us to go deep into constitutional convolutions. I think there is a slight danger of our erecting a theological dispute over one of the narrowest ideological divides in the history of politics. A good deal has been heard and written about the SDP in the past few weeks, but too much has been about structure and not enough about objectives. Let us get this argument into proportion. Of course it would be foolish to seek a premature and therefore disruptive merger. It could be damaging to have a continuing time-consuming argument about this. But do not set a limit to the march of the Alliance. Do not try to impose too many rules or bans or prescriptions on local parties from the centre. If the Alliance is to grow closer, which it must, it is best that it should do so organically, on the ground, from the bottom up.

Beyond that let us remember one crucial precept. The SDP is in substantial part a revolt against the presumptions of party politics and party politicians: against the view that it is the inward audience that matters; against the view that so long as you abuse the other side loud enough it does not matter whether you make sense to the public; against the view that a party as such is a sacred tabernacle, however squalid may be the contortions which go on upon its floor. It is this approach which first poisoned and is now killing the Labour Party. Parties, including the SDP, are not an end in themselves. They should exist not for their own sakes, but for the effect they can have on the political health of a nation and the aspirations of its people.

That political health is not strong today. We have a Government confirmed in its faults by the ease of its victory; with its dogmatism increased by the spurious size of its parliamentary majority. Yet its real strength in share of the electorate is no more than that secured by Mr Heath in his nadir year of 1966. We have an official opposition which is about to proclaim its renunciation of government by compounding unacceptable policies with a totally inexperienced leadership.

Yet the aspirations are there: the need for an enlightened far-sighted internationalism; the need to revive the economy, which has fallen again, even more exhausted by the election and the bogus claims then made for it than were the politicians; the need for a rational defence of our continuously threatened public services; the need for fairness without regimentation.

It is a tailor-made opportunity for our new leader, with his experience of government, his unique ability to seize the issue of the moment and synthesise it into a longer-term perspective. Working in the closest alliance with our essential and respected Liberal partners, I believe that we can enthuse the nation and astonish the world even more than we did in 1981. And this time our advance will take us over the threshold of victory and will stick. That is our task. Let us get on with it.

PART TWO

GENERAL PRINCIPLES

CHAPTER I

The Economy and Unemployment

In Part One I set out to show the birth and establishment of the SDP, and then the Alliance, through Roy Jenkins' speeches and articles. In Part Two I have grouped his articles and speeches under subjects, rather than putting them in a generally chronological order.

Of course Roy Jenkins made other speeches and wrote other articles but the subjects that follow largely suggested themselves. These were subjects that were the very cornerstones of the new Social Democratic Party: Constitutional Reform; Defence; Unemployment; Europe. Attitudes to these issues go far towards explaining the philosophy of Social Democracy.

It would be unthinkable in making such a selection not to include subjects in which Roy Jenkins had immense and unquestionable authority based on high office: Europe from the ex-President of the EEC; the death penalty from a man who was twice Home Secretary. But at the core of politics lies economics. In the seventies and eighties, with Conservative and Labour alike pursuing their economic ideologies with little success, the statements and attitudes of a great former Chancellor of the Exchequer setting out the approach of the Alliance to British economic policy is, I believe, a matter of true significance.

British Economic Policy Revisited

The first subjects I have chosen are the economy and unemployment.

On 23 February 1981 Roy Jenkins spoke to the Institute of Fiscal Studies at the Royal Society of Arts. Lord Croham (Sir Douglas Allen), who had been his permanent Secretary at the Treasury from 1968 to 1970, was in the chair.

Anyone returning to this country after four years of substantial if not complete absence is bound to be dismayed by the economic scene. I simply do not understand the attitude of those who believe that behind the facade of falling production and mounting unemployment something triumphant is occurring. There are certain fields in which, according to one's beliefs, a purification of the spirit may be achieved through a mortification of the flesh. The management of economic policy is not one of them. It is essentially a material process using material means to achieve material ends. Its success is to be judged by wealth-creating results and not by moral purpose and/or virility tests. 'Let wealth and commerce, laws and learning die. But give us back our old virility', to paraphrase two of the silliest lines in English poetry, is not a very good economic motto.

Of course it is reasonable that success should be judged by developments over a period and not merely by a snapshot of the position on a particular day. Of course it is the case that some fairly deep-seated evils, for example the tendency of the economy to absorb a given degree of stimulus more in price than in output increases, have been developing for a long time. Of course it is the case that we live in a much more difficult world climate than was the case ten — or still more — twenty years ago. But it should also be remembered that we are more insulated against one of the major causes of that difficulty — expensive and uncertain oil — than any of the other countries who attend Western Economic summits, except for Canada, the smallest economy of the seven. Yet we, almost the most feather-bedded in this important respect, have produced the worst recession of all the Organisation for Economic Co-operation and Development (OECD) countries, indeed so far as industrial output is concerned the deepest recession, I believe, to have been seen in any major industrial country since the war — a drop of about fourteen per cent over two years. The only qualification to that remark is that if we go on much longer as we are doing we shall soon cease to qualify as a major industrial country. In five years' time on present trends South Korea will be a greater industrial power than Britain.

Now conceivably all this could be justified if we were undergoing a short-term purge the debilitating effects of which would automatically cease at a certain point and from which long-term gains would demonstrably follow. I would certainly pay a heavy short-term price if as a result significant inflation could be permanently extracted from the system. But I do not see that happening. The losses are manifest and are permanent, first in the obvious sense that any two or three years' loss of production once it has occurred is a loss for ever, but also in the more special sense that we are now on or over the threshold of the permanent loss of major productive capacities, the permanent closing down of export lines. But what about the permanence of the gains and indeed their scale? Inflation is falling — from a very high level. It has still some distance to go before even the parabola in the sky is complete — before we are back where this Government began. I am no great admirer of the economic policies of the last Labour Government, although I think that, with a little help from the International Monetary Fund (IMF), they began to get better after I left it. I like to believe that was *post hoc* rather than *propter hoc.* Then they deteriorated again with and after the

Budget of 1978. That Government did however get the inflation rate rather unstably below ten per cent. This is just about what I think this Government will do, but with a great deal more help from the exchange rate and with many other penalties as well. But I see only very limited reasons to think that it would necessarily be a more permanent achievement than that of 1978-9, such as that was. This will be very far from a major extrusion of inflation from the system. I believe economic management is a question of the balancing of risks. Sometimes the risks on one side are much greater than those on the other. I used to like a simile which compared running the economy with riding a bicycle along a narrow path half way up a cliff. If you got it wrong one way you had a nasty bruise on your elbow. If you got it wrong the other you fell 300 feet. In these circumstances it was obvious what the bias of your steering should be.

I now see it rather differently. In a way the risk of sudden catastrophe has been removed. The path has gone off the cliff into a different terrain. I suppose that is a result — for ten years or so — of the oil. The danger now is that you chase an elusive butterfly without noticing that you have gone down into a deep valley from which, without capturing the butterfly, you find that you have lost the strength to ride up again.

Looking back over ten or eleven years I feel some responsibility for having hatched the butterfly. You will recall that in 1969-70 we had a negative Public Sector Borrowing Requirement (PSBR). We repaid Government debt to the extent of about £450 million — about £1.5 billion at today's prices. This was the only year for decades in which this was so, although Stafford Cripps got near to a similar performance at the end of the forties. Labour — or perhaps I should say Social Democratic Chancellors — can be more prudent financiers than Conservative ones. But that PSBR position must be seen in context. It was accompanied by a balance of payments surplus, an inflation rate of 5.8 per cent, unemployment under 600,000 and a growth rate of about 2½ per cent. Moreover industry and construction then provided employment for 9.7 million people. Today the only thing which is common is the balance of payments surplus. For the rest we have inflation at thirteen per cent, unemployment at 2.4 million, growth well below zero, and employment in manufacturing and construction down to 7.5 million people. But in these totally different circumstances the flickering attraction of that negative PSBR has, I believe, exercised a considerable and dangerous attraction upon the leader of the present Government. In the early days I believe she thought she could get back there. But what she has so far succeeded in doing, with perverse and damaging side-effects, has been to put it up from about £6 billion to around £13 billion. As the hatcher of the butterfly, I can perhaps be excused from the charge of being a profligate financier. But the plain fact is that, without a revolutionary destruction of the assumptions of the modern state you cannot reduce the Public Sector Borrowing Requirement in conditions of recessions. You cannot escape the effect on the Government spending on unemployment — a direct cost of £3,500 a man and a direct and indirect cost of nearer £6,000 and of high interest rates — nor the effect on government revenue of falling profits and disappearing income. And the harder you push the deeper you get into the mud.

The fundamental fault of this Government is not that it takes account of the money supply. Any sensible person recognises that an adequate regard for the money supply is an important part of economic management. But it must, like other indicators, be kept in its place. Much of the dispute between Keynesianism and monetarism is rather sterile. What surely matters, and what is desirable to get right, is total spending of money: Gross Domestic Product (GDP) — 'nominal GDP' in America. What is foolish is to try to move it one way with the right hand of fiscal policy and the other way with the left hand of monetary policy. The two ought clearly to pull together, although what is perhaps still more important is that they should pull together in the right direction and with the right strength according to the circumstances of the time and the balance of objectives which you wish to achieve; and that is no more than sensible Keynesianism, or if you like moderate monetarism.

The criticism of this Government is not that it has sought to have a monetary dial amongst its controls, but that it has had only one when it ought to have had several for this purpose alone — the Federal Reserve has five, I believe — and that it has paid too much attention to a single crude and flickering instrument which has not responded to its touch, and which in any event ought not to be looked at in isolation but in relation to a whole series of other panels. Any modern economy, even one as sluggish as the British one has recently proved to be, is a complicated affair. To try to fly it on one instrument is like trying to fly a Jumbo Jet on a small car's speedometer. In the circumstances it is a wonder that we are still aloft at all. The fact that even after recent zigzags we are still going pretty hard in the wrong direction is not encouraging, but at least means that we have the opportunity to turn round before disaster.

In what direction should we turn? The central issue is how we deal with the years of oil abundance in order to leave ourselves in the best possible position to live without the oil in the future. This is a medium-term approach which demands a stability of policy over a substantial period. We simply cannot afford to go on with sudden lurches of policy, with denationalisation or renationalisation, each without bringing in a penny of fresh capital or creating a single new job. Equally damaging are sudden switches of demand management policy. And these have occurred only too frequently in the past, not only as a result of changes of government every four or five years or six years, but also as a result of governments spending the second half of their life trying to undo the harm they have done, often because of manifesto commitments, in the first half. We thus live in something approaching a two-year syndrome of damaging fluctuation. One of the strong arguments for electoral reform and indeed for political realignment is to get away from this queasy big-dipper ride.

To return to the substance of the matter, let us examine how North Sea oil can affect the economy. To illustrate the problem let us take the extreme and fanciful hypothesis that we decided to use the entire oil reserve to finance a two-year holiday for the whole population. That is about what it is worth. We would all have to go to the sun as no one would be working in Britain, not even hotel keepers. Manifestly when we came back our factories would have rusted and our markets disappeared and the nation would be permanently and desperately impoverished. This is clearly fanciful, but there is a quarter-way house which is much nearer to what we in fact are in danger of doing: consuming (rather than investing) half the oil over say a seven-year period, and doing so by paying ourselves about twenty per cent above the international value of our work and each year sending an additional five per cent of the labour force to an involuntary holiday at home — known as unemployment. Then at the end of the seven years our position, while not as obviously cataclysmic as with the first fanciful hypothesis would nonetheless be pretty desperate. We would face a major fall in real national income. This is not to say that we should not pay for some consumption out of the oil or to deny that its exploitation is bound to have some effect on the rest of our economy. But should we combine our oil advantage with a dogmatic monetarism at home and a disregard for the exchange rate abroad which has and is generating a massive economy, not to mention unrealistic rates against the dollar and the ECU.

The effect of the oil, combined with natural trends in mature industrial societies, no doubt means some de-industrialisation, but what this should mean is a successful industrialised nation gradually shifting its place in the international division of labour towards more employment in jobs of high skill and pay, in design, in high value-added services, in innovative and advanced technology. These activites should be integrated with a strong and viable industrial sector. But this is not what is happening. The industrial heartlands of Britain are not transforming their employment along these lines. The problems are great enough for Norway, which has about as much oil as we have, but only a twentieth of the population. We have to employ a labour force of about $24\frac{1}{2}$ million people, alongside the 50,000 to 100,000 who are employed in oil and gas extraction. If we fail to

F

get a proper balance here, which requires a cautious depletion policy but many other things as well, we may soon come to curse the oil rather than treating it as the first economic bonus we have had for several decades.

It is essential that we use a large part of the oil revenue for productive public sector investment; railway electrification, public transport generally, the expansion of British Telecom, energy saving and insulation work, the development of renewable resources, the renewal of outdated water and sewerage systems. This would be of great benefit to the construction industry, which is near to its knees. In spite of the traditional objections to the hypothecation of revenue, a special North Sea Oil Revenue Investment Fund may be the right way to proceed here.

Private sector profitability and investment also needs a boost. It is a particular irony that the policies of the present Government seem not only to be involuntarily increasing the proportions of the national income taken by public expenditure but also to be weakening the private sector, large parts of which have no safety net, more than the public sector. The best help that can be given here is through cuts in interest rates and downward pressure on the exchange rate. Such measures would be more sensible, comprehensive and effective than a battery of *ad hoc* measures such as import controls, cuts in particular energy prices or special hand-outs to firms about to go bankrupt. Import controls need to be approached with particular caution. Quite a number of them already exist at the level of the European Community, in substantial part introduced at British behest. Do not let us deceive ourselves into the belief that import controls are an effective way out. To the extent that they escaped retaliation they would tend to push up the exchange rate rather than bring it down. But over the lifespan of any investment cycle in the present uncertain climate of world trade, they would be bound to invite retaliation. Let us for a moment sit back and think how weak is the case for import controls by an oil-rich industrialised country with a balance of payments surplus. We would enjoy no world sympathy. We would inevitably be subject to retaliation, not only from resource-poor, over-indebted developing countries, but also from other industrialised countries with balance of payments deficits and no oil.

I therefore believe that we should go for lower interest rates and a lower exchange rate. We cannot wholly control the latter, but we could have a substantial effect upon it. The exchange rate will in any event come down in due course. It is much better that we should try to bring it gradually down now, rather than let it collapse later, when large parts of our manufacturing industry will have already collapsed, and in many cases irrevocably so. We should also mount a major programme of public infrastructure investment, directly related to the flow into the Exchequer of oil revenue.

Can we relate this to a tolerable anti-inflation policy? If we are to favour employment with lower interest and exchange rates, and not restimulate inflation with a wild relaxation of money supply or credit growth, as in 1972-3, then we have to go back to the pursuit of a stability-orientated incomes policy. And if we want, as I do, as decentralised and unbureaucratic an economy as possible, we must do this without tying ourselves up in regulatory knots. Nor do we want something which will only serve a short-term purpose. We want something which will serve us for a period of years, improving on our present appallingly bad mix of unemployment, inflation and inefficiency, and yet leaving as much flexibility as possible in pay bargaining. This could mean a variety of techniques for making inflationary behaviour less rewarding in the short run and agreeing on circumstances in which only a minority of disputed claims would be subjected to mandatory settlement.

Amongst the most interesting of the ideas put forward are those of Professor James Meade, of which the core is an employment-oriented Pay Commission, which would not involve itself with any freely agreed bargain, but which would be open for business from any party to a disagreed wage settlement. The Commission would, subject to various limitations, judge a settlement at either the employees' last claim or the employers' last offer, whichever would be more likely to favour employment in the enterprises concerned. Enforcement would be not through the full panoply of the criminal law, but through a weakening of a potential striker's financial position in the realm of tax rebates, supplementary benefits, redundancy conditions. In a setting of high unemployment and weak competitivity such a system would clearly favour wage moderation; in sectoral or company situations of labour shortage, it would also be satisfactorily flexible. I am less sure how it would work in a more generally tight labour market, but that is at present some distance away from us. I do not pretend to a complete answer, but I think this offers the right direction.

In fact there are rarely complete, one hundred per cent watertight answers to economic problems. In the rather slovenly phrase the best can indeed be the enemy of the good. Looking for perfection can prevent sensible changes carrying a good chance of success. But the present mix is something very near to disaster. It will not destroy inflation, although at a great price it may modify it. It will permanently damage a large part of our economy and it will make the worst rather than the best use of the limited period when the oil is in flood.

Can We Improve the Economy?

Speaking to the Council for Social Democracy on 9 October 1981 at the Central Hall in Westminster, Roy Jenkins made a series of positive suggestions.

We have had years of relative economic decline. But the depression into which this country has been plunged by this incompetently dogmatic Government is beyond that. It now bears in many respects direct and even unfavourable comparison with the Great Depression of the early 1930s.

Between 1929 and 1931 National Income fell by six per cent and industrial production by ten per cent. Since June 1979 National Income has fallen by seven per cent and industrial production by almost twenty per cent. In 1932 unemployment exceeded three million but then fell to $1\frac{3}{4}$ million by 1937. In late 1981 and 1982 unemployment will similarly exceed three million. But by contrast with 1932 there is now no prospect of a rapid and steady fall after that. The Government's Chief Economic Adviser has told us that. On the contrary, there is, on present policies, a likelihood of it continuing to rise until the mid-1980s. By then it could well match, not only in absolute numbers but as a percentage of the working population — not of course in absolute poverty, for we must not exaggerate — the worst experience of the thirties. The prospects of work for the three million unemployed are worse in 1981 than they were in 1931.

A short time ago few of us would have believed this possible. It is not true, as the Government sometimes claims, that we are the inevitable victims of a world recession. Others are suffering too, but we, who because of North Sea oil should be the most insulated, are suffering the worst. In industrial production it is the deepest recession experienced by any advanced country since the war.

Nor is it true, as a second and contradictory alibi, that North Sea oil, through its effects on the exchange rate, necessarily involved this degree of de-industrialisation. Norway, with a relatively bigger 'oil impact', has by sensible management kept its unemployment under two per cent.

We have been driven from the doldrums into near disaster by the policies which this Government has deliberately chosen to pursue. Why? They may be foolish but they are not insane. They may be uncaring, but they do not seek electoral defeat. They have persuaded themselves that the only remedy is to seek to control inflation by an excessive concentration, although at the same time an often incompetent concentration, upon the money supply.

How do we get out of this impasse? Can this Government possibly lead us out? I wish they could, for the seriousness of the situation transcends all party interest. But they cannot, and essentially for one simple reason. They have utterly failed to learn an obvious lesson. Their central policy cannot succeed without reducing the Public Sector Borrowing Requirement. And that cannot be done in any acceptable way in conditions of recession. The budgetary costs of unemployment, £3,500 a man direct, nearer £7,000 indirectly, and the interest rate costs too, mean that they are trying to walk up an escalator which is going down with greater energy than they can command. Uncomprehending and misdirected effort is self-defeating.

Can the Conservative critics do it? Their analyses are admirable, their remedies are sensible, but so long as they remain anxious to wound but afraid to strike, their performance will be lamentable. Mr Du Cann, who has sense, has criticised Mr Heath, who has wisdom, for not doing it all privately. No doubt he would have criticised the geese of Rome for not squawking quietly. I pray that the old rigidities of party loyalties which have for too long made monkeys of too many of us will not force the Tory critics back into supine muttering accompanied no doubt by attacks on us in order to re-establish their party credentials.

And the Labour Party? When it has time, which is rare, it fulminates against the Government, but it fulminates without impact. First, even the old pre-1979 Labour Party did a good deal to pave the way towards our present descent. But, much more important, its present remedies offer the illusion of utopia without the reality even of amelioration.

Its attitude to public finance would debase the currency. Its nationalisation proposals would snuff out such vestiges of confidence as still remain in the private sector on which most jobs depend. Its narrow protectionism not only nullifies its protestations of concern for the Third World, but would also enshrine our declining competitiveness and invite retaliation from our industrial partners. What chance do they think there is of an oil-rich country, with a balance of payments surplus, asking countries in deficit without any oil, to accept this lying down? And its policy of abrupt withdrawal from the European Community, to the other countries of which, with their trade associates, now go fifty-eight per cent of our exports, is a recipe not for creating jobs but for throwing another million people out of work.

Therefore an immense responsibility devolves upon us. What should we do, what can we do, realistically, without promising to the British people what we cannot deliver, a course against which this Party must resolutely set its face?

We need a three-phase operation. First, a reversal of the trend and a significant reduction of unemployment in the short term. Second, the rekindling of economic growth on a steady and sustainable basis. Third, the restructuring of the economy, through measures to strengthen our industrial and exporting base against the day, not too far ahead, when the flow of the North Sea oil begins to ebb.

On the first point, I set out during the Warrington campaign a carefully costed six-point crash programme for reducing unemployment by one million over one to two years at an annual cost of between £2 and £3 billion. It was designed to have the maximum impact on unemployment for the minimum increase in public expenditure. Its arithmetic has never been challenged, not even by our complacent Chancellor, who came to Warrington just a few days later, exactly when he would, if they could have worked one out, have tried to present a counter-attacking Treasury brief. The effect of the six-point plan on the PSBR would have been less than his last year's margin of error. It was based on the view that the way to deal with this real problem of the PSBR was to pull back and take a run at it rather than to dig deeper into failure.

It is a small risk well worth taking in present circumstances. Such a programme could also have a follow-through repercussive effect and create still more jobs. But the crash programme contains some palliatives and subsidies. It needs to be overtaken by more medium-term and less artificially kindled growth.

This depends essentially on two points. First, confidence in both the public and private sectors of industry. To this we can make a unique contribution. The Tories consider the public sector an albatross round their necks, and the Labour Party look on the private sector, with its enterprise, initiative and profits, as an excrescence on the centralised economy and the flat surface of controlled mediocrity. For God's sake let us have an end to the futile frontier war between public and private sectors; let us have stability and respect for both. And let us have understanding, so dismally lacking in both major parties today, for the problems of businessmen and managers trying to make decisions.

Second, there is the problem of taking off the brakes on expansion without further rekindling inflation. Previous governments have used centrally imposed incomes policies, either by intention or by lurch. This has worked for short periods — but inadequately from our point of view for two reasons: the methods were too bureaucratic and centralised and too short-term. How do we overcome this? I think one of the most interesting and worthwhile proposals for us to study urgently and intensively is that for an inflation tax.

We need to have prior discussion between the Government and the trades unions. We want the unions to play a full part in their proper industrial job, and not too great a part in their improper role of political king-makers, to which the increasingly bizarre constitution of the Labour Party has more and more elevated them.

After discussion the Government would announce guidance on the rate of growth of average hourly earnings the country could afford over the coming year. If an employer increased the average hourly earnings of his employees by more than this, the excess payments would be subject to a tax. If, for example, the tax rate was fifty per cent then for every pound paid above the recommended rate, the firm would have to pay an extra fifty pence in tax. The tax would be relatively straightforward to collect. In addition, it should be possible at the end of the year to reduce the rate of National Insurance Surcharge to balance previous inflation tax payments and thereby ensure that the tax burden on the company sector as a whole would not increase. Firms paying more than the country could afford would be penalised: others would positively benefit.

Such a tax would not stamp out inflation but it would effectively restrain the wage-price spiral in the private sector. If then — and this is essential — public sector payments were fairly related to pay in the private sector, the restraining influence of the tax would be felt throughout the economy. And as the vicious process of wages following prices and prices following wages was damped down in this way, it would become possible for the new Social Democratic/Liberal Government to revive expansionary forces in the economy and set unemployment on a permanently downward path.

This approach has a number of substantial advantages in line with the principles of social democracy. First the new tax structure would be permanent and stable. It would avoid the 'on-off' phases of previous incomes policies, and as its success built up it would be extremely unlikely that any government would abandon it. Second, the guiding rate would be encouraged by an incentive but not enforced by a *Diktat*, so that firms with a pressing need to acquire more labour would be able to do so — at a price. Third, free collective bargaining would go on: there would be no question of interference from the centre in individual agreements freely negotiated. It is a practical example of the way in which social democratic principles, properly applied, could help to resolve one of the most intractable problems of our nation.

My third point is on the need for a major long-term programme for the re-equipment of our industry — perhaps the creation of a North Sea Oil fund. This would not make any more money available, but it would remind us of the impermanence of our oil. Few things are more disturbing than the collapse of capital expenditure, both public and private. The volume of government spending on fixed capital formation has fallen from an index figure of 100 in 1970 to 39 today, with 37 projected for next year. The same trend is at work in private industry: investment has been frozen out by a lack of prospect of profitability which prevents the surmounting of high interest rates. This trend must be reversed. A Fund could be used to assist such a process in both the public and — by making money available at significantly reduced rates of interest — in the private sector. The decision as to when and in what form to invest in the private sector must be left to those who bear the responsibility for success or failure and can judge the market prospects, but as in many of our competitor countries the state can improve the conditions within which these decisions are taken.

Such an approach offers us the possibility of a major immediate reduction in unemployment, with strong follow-through effects. These, combined with the medium-term proposals, and the big demographic change which is bound to occur from about 1985, transform the position after the middle of the decade. I do not agree with the hopeless, inevitable permanent view about unemployment.

We can also bring inflation sufficiently under control to prevent it being the enemy of growth; and create the prospect for the nineties of a strong and robust economy which can live with and surmount the decline and loss of oil revenues.

These are not small or easy achievements. There is no hope of them either on present policies or with the wild remedies of the Labour Party. The new approach, the practical but undogmatic remedies, the appeal across the interests, across the classes, across the nation, the stability of direction, is essential.

Is there a contradiction between wanting both radical change and greater stability of political direction? No. We believe in change which will stick, because it springs from the needs of the nation and not from outdated dogmas or tired manifestos. That is in the great tradition of radical responsible reform, which has been dead for too long and to which we are the true heirs.

Hillhead: Proposals for Employment

On 4 March 1982 at Hillhead, three weeks before polling day, Roy Jenkins set out a practical approach to unemployment.

It is now undeniable that the recession which has gathered pace over the last two-and-a-half years has been the worst to afflict the British economy since the Great Depression of 1929-31. Since the middle of 1979, national income has fallen by about seven per cent in real terms and manufacturing production by about twenty per cent — rather worse than the experience fifty years ago. Total unemployment now exceeds three million for the first time since 1932 — one million jobs have been lost in manufacturing industry, and adult unemployment has risen from 1.2 million (five per cent) in the autumn of 1979 to well over 2.7 million (over eleven per cent) now. Experience in Scotland has been directly parallel with, but somewhat worse than that of Britain as a whole: unemployment here has now risen to over 325,000, or thirteen-and-a-half per cent on a seasonally-adjusted basis. It is still worse in the West of Scotland, the area which in the past made the greatest contribution to Britain's economic greatness.

One does not have to be a wild radical to say that faced with figures of this order, unemployment is by far the greatest problem facing Britain today, and that it must be the top priority of a new government to turn the tide of our national economic decline and start to get the jobless back to work. I want tonight to explain how an SDP/Liberal Alliance Government would set about tackling the unemployment problem. I want to illustrate the benefits which a new approach to economic management could bring by setting out the sort of programme which I recommend in current circumstances.

I can claim to be a prudent financier. I was the only one of the now thirteen post-war Chancellors actually to reduce government debt — in sharp contrast with Sir Geoffrey Howe's record of increasing it by £33 billion. But I did it when circumstances made it right and compatible with keeping unemployment below 600,000 and inflation at little more than five per cent. I also put our balance of payments firmly into credit and paid back overseas as well as internal debts. But different circumstances demand different measures. It is no good, to quote Keynes's famous example, having a parrot which says 'Oh, what a lovely morning', however hard the wind is blowing and the rain is pouring down. That is what Sir Geoffrey Howe is near to becoming.

We need a programme to get us out of today's pattern of industrial decline. Such a programme would, I believe, reduce unemployment by over a million within two years. Neither of the two old parties offers realistic hope. A large part of our current troubles is directly attributable to Government policies, and there is no sign that those policies will improve. Mrs Thatcher likes to say that unemployment is unavoidable on account of the world recession. But if this were true, the recession here would be at worst similar in extent to that being suffered by other industrial countries, and at best less, because the existence of North Sea oil should have helped us to withstand the 1979 price shock. In fact it is much worse, and it is much worse mainly because of the Government's ineffective but damaging obsession with public borrowing. This has caused them to fly in the face of economic reason by taking a whole series

of measures which have made both unemployment and inflation worse
— cutting Rate Support Grant which has put up rates and council house
rents, increasing VAT and other indirect taxes, raising interest rates,
forcing nationalised industries' prices, particularly gas, to well above the
economic level. As unemployment has risen and the Government has
resorted to more and more of the same medicine, higher interest rates
have pushed the pound up to uncompetitive levels on the foreign
exchanges and made the squeeze on industry still worse. The loss of jobs
from now near-bankrupt companies that until recently were perfectly
sound and profitable has become a cascade.

And what has it all been for? To reduce inflation? Let there be no
fudging of the plain fact that inflation is now two points higher, at twelve
per cent, than it was when the Government came into office. And there is
no early prospect of it falling significantly below the ten per cent of May
1979. We pay the price but we do not get the benefit. To lay a basis for
recovery? But why should recovery come when the economy has been
weakened by two years' deflation on this scale, when profitability has
never been lower, and when the combination of high inflation and a high
exchange rate has produced a massive loss of competitiveness?

The truth is that unless the Government acts, and acts decisively, there
will be no significant economic recovery, and an unemployment rate in
excess of three million will be with us indefinitely. This is not just a
politician's claim. It is borne out by all the main economic forecasts,
whether their approach be 'monetarist' or 'Keynesian'. Assuming a
continuation of present policies the 'Keynesian' National Institute of
Economic and Social Research expects economic growth to stay, at least
until 1986, well below the level needed to bring any reduction in
unemployment. The projections of the 'monetarist' London Business
School, allegedly on Mrs Thatcher's side, tell the same dismal story. The
independent Manpower Services Commission has said it would not
expect major reductions below three million over the next five years.

What then should be done? There is no economic salvation at the end
of the route mapped out by Labour. Their policies would compound the
economic catastrophe. They propose a combination of massive increases
in public expenditure — wild figures adding £20 billion or more to the
PSBR are bandied about — further nationalisation, price controls and
import controls following withdrawal from the EEC. And all this with
hardly a word about the need to restrain incomes if inflation is to be
contained — a subject which is anathema to the trades union barons on
whose support they rely. One does not have to be an economic expert to
see the consequences of the policies they are putting forward. Massive
increases in spending without effective incomes policies would generate

massive inflation and debauch the currency. The loss of jobs, rising steadily as inflation once gathered pace, would be turned into a flood as price controls were imposed and companies' profits destroyed by wage pressure on the one hand and price ceilings on the other. Withdrawal from the EEC and import controls, against the background of the huge balance of payments advantage afforded to our country by self-sufficiency in oil, would precipitate massive retaliation by our trading partners and more unemployment as more markets were lost. Far from presenting a solution to the unemployment problem, I believe Labour's recipe would make it immeasurably worse.

But there is no reason to despair. A determined attack on the unemployment problem can be made, and can be made to succeed, provided we approach it rationally and shake off the unreasoning dogma which consistently blinds the judgement of those in the two old parties. Whereas Mrs Thatcher has asserted, against all the evidence of the last thirty years, that it is not within the power of governments to influence the unemployment rate, except very temporarily, I say that an Alliance Government can and will take vigorous action to set unemployment on a downward trend. Whereas Mrs Thatcher asserts that fiscal and monetary policies should not be used to counter a recession — and in fact has used them to make it worse — I say that it is right for the government's borrowing, and for that matter the money supply, to rise somewhat in a recession, provided that adverse inflationary consequences can be avoided.

Whereas Mrs Thatcher's Chief Economic Adviser has declared that 'the nation will have to be patient', I say that it is unacceptable to offer the unemployed no hope until the end of the decade. The Government must act now.

I propose, in line with but in more detail than what has hitherto been proposed by the SDP, an emergency programme of special measures specifically designed to achieve the maximum reduction in unemployment quickly and at minimum cost. It takes proper note of the Manpower Services Commission's (MSC) recent report which drew particular attention to the plight of the long-term unemployed, the young unemployed, and married women. The numbers of the long-term unemployed have been rising disproportionately so that over a million people will soon have been registered as unemployed for a year or more, one-and-a-half million for six months or more, and people in this longer-term category are forecast to represent over fifty per cent of all those unemployed at least to 1986. They also drew special attention to school leavers. In their case even the package of special employment measures announced last July and a slight reduction in the numbers of school-leaving age are unlikely to outweigh the general reduction in employment opportunities for the under-eighteen age group.

I therefore propose a crash employment programme, targeted on these particular groups, consisting of the following measures:

First, I repeat the proposal which I put forward last July to boost jobs in the private sector by paying a £70 a week grant to every employer taking on an additional worker who has been unemployed for over six months. This scheme is for employment pay, not unemployment pay. The money for the grant would otherwise go to keep the man unemployed. The company's workforce would be monitored to ensure that there was no reduction in non-subsidised employment. Public expenditure would still rise somewhat, because the grant would unavoidably be paid for some new jobs that would have been created in any event, but at a net PSBR cost of around £2,000 a year for each job, the price of roughly £500 million would be well worth paying for the 250,000 jobs the scheme could generate.

Second, to combat the sense of waste and frustration which so many of them feel, I believe that it should be possible to offer the long-term unemployed a job guarantee, if they wish to take it up. People are always saying: 'Why do we pay people to do nothing, when there is so much to be done?' And they are right. There is a multitude of things which the long-term unemployed could be well employed in doing. The jobs to back the guarantee would be made available in a national campaign of housing and environmental improvement — things like house insulation to reduce fuel consumption for the nation and fuel bills for the individual, house repairs and improvement, clearing derelict sites, improving pavements, or tending the parks — all activities where the costs of materials are low, the needs great (not least in the West of Scotland), and where many of the unemployed have at least the basic skills. People taking part would be paid a bonus (perhaps £15 per week) above their social benefits; the scheme would be organised by the Manpower Services Commission, drawing as necessary on the expertise in the private sector and local councils; and the clients, both public and private, would be required to pay something for the services, though perhaps not much more than the cost of the materials. In addition there would be a large expansion in the Community Enterprise Programme for adults, which provides similar work opportunities useful to the community, and where the net cost per job is only about £1,500. In total another 250,000 jobs could be provided in these ways at a net cost to the PSBR not exceeding £500 million.

Third, there should be special measures to encourage youth employment. A slump hits youth employment harder than adult employment, particularly where vocational training is as deficient as it is in Britain. Since the youth labour market has become the soggiest of all markets, it is the least inflationary to stimulate. And there is of course an investment for the future element in youth employment. It is worth spending a good deal to get the youth labour market going again, for otherwise the Exchequer cost of the Youth Training Scheme — due to be extended to all unemployed school leavers in 1983 — will become enormous: it now costs around £60 per week per person. And it is better to provide jobs with training than rather haphazard training without the prospect of jobs. I propose that employers should be offered a £30 a week subsidy for every youth they employ under the age of eighteen, and that the major training requirement should be linked to this. The time has come to follow the German example with a requirement that every worker under eighteen be provided with at least eight hours formal training a week off the job. The cost of these proposals would be around £600 million above the alternative costs of guaranteeing all unemployed young people a one-year place on the Youth Training Scheme. The proposals should lead to the creation of about a quarter of a million new jobs. Since many of the young people assisted by the subsidy would otherwise have been on training programmes, the actual reduction in unemployment would probably not exceed 50,000, but the full programme to put 250,000 young people in jobs rather than training, which so often seems purposeless, would be well worthwhile.

Fourth, to improve the employment position of women, who are particularly hard-hit in a recession, we should increase spending on certain vital services which rely heavily on female labour. Home helps are real value for money. They assist old people to live at home and not become dependent on, but often less happy in, more costly residental care. It would cost about £200 million to provide 60,000 women with part-time jobs in such activities.

This emergency programme would reduce unemployment by some 610,000 at a net cost of less than £1½ billion on the PSBR. The gross cost is somewhat higher, but the net addition to the PSBR is small because the alternative of paying people to be unemployed is so costly — about £4,500 a year per person — and because higher tax revenues, both because of higher profits and higher incomes, follow from a higher level of economic activity. It is a sensible programme to provide jobs where so much needs to be done, and to pay people for being employed rather than unemployed, and it would work.

In addition to this short-term programme to bring unemployment down quickly, an Alliance Government would wish to take general measures of a fiscal and monetary kind to get the economy moving again, provided that these did not lead to undue inflationary pressures. The guiding principle here should be to adopt expansionary measures which simultaneously exert a downward pressure on the price level — the opposite of the Government's approach which has been to adopt depressing measures which simultaneously put prices up.

I propose the following budgetary package, the effects of which have been worked out from the Treasury's own economic model.

First, a major reduction to one-and-a-half per cent of the National Insurance Surcharge. This is a tax on employment at a time of high unemployment and reduces industry's competitiveness in overseas markets. Its reduction would encourage exports and reduce costs, and according to Treasury estimates would increase gross domestic product by about 0.6 per cent, reduce prices by over half a per cent and bring unemployment down by about 50,000 at a net cost of about £1 billion on the PSBR. Complete abolition with an approximate doubling of these effects is the alternative. I would not rule this out, and would in any event try to achieve it in two stages.

Second, I propose an increase in public capital expenditure of about £2½ billion of which approximately £1½ billion will be a net charge on the PSBR. One of the most disturbing features of the past decade has been the fall in the proportion of capital spending within the total of public expenditure from 20% to 8%. This is desperately dangerous for the future. Much of my proposed increase should be concentrated on *construction,* since one in eight of the unemployed are associated with the construction industry, and construction projects are particularly labour intensive. I propose an increase in spending on house-building of about £1½ billion, to provide for rehabilitation and modernisation of older council estates and blocks — which would be particularly valuable in Glasgow — an increase in improvement grants and substantially increased funds for Housing Associations. I would supplement this housing effort with additional investment of about £500 million in small civil engineering projects and other works such as improvements to the sewerage and drainage systems and road projects offering environmental benefits. This construction programme taken as a whole could create an additional 250,000 jobs at a *net* cost to the PSBR of about £1 billion.

As a further addition to useful public capital spending, I would permit some relaxation in nationalised industries' cash limits to take place where this is demonstrably worthwhile. It is ludicrous, for example, that highly profitable investment in telecommunications should he held back at this time. If good investment of this kind were permitted to go ahead, at a net cost to the PSBR of about £500 million, another 50,000 jobs would be generated.

Third, as part of our general willingness to operate fiscal and monetary policies counter-cyclically provided that no serious inflationary consequences follow, an Alliance Government should allow the money supply to expand a little more quickly than under present plans, and keep interest rates rather lower. This would imply a rather lower exchange rate, with a consequential expansionary effect on the economy. A rather less restrictive monetary stance would not have much effect on the Retail Price Index, but it could have a worthwhile impact on employment at the same time as helping to reduce the PSBR by reducing debt interest. The Treasury's illustrative figures, for example, show that a two per cent drop in interest rates would be associated with a drop of over £1 billion in the PSBR, and 65,000 more jobs. Choosing prudently but not dogmatically, the right rate for monetary expansion would therefore be an important part of our policy.

A budgetary package on these lines would give a significant upward push to the level of national income, without a significant impact on the rate of inflation, because some parts would help bring it down, and could reduce unemployment by a further 450,000 at a net PSBR cost of just over £2½ billion.

Taking the programme of measures as a whole, unemployment could be reduced by over a million within two years, at a net cost to the PSBR of the order of £4 billion. This is over and above measures to restore income tax thresholds, which I assume that even the Chancellor will do in any event, and without which the Budget would not be neutral but would drive us further into deflation. Much other discussion of the issues gives the less relevant gross costs and is not therefore directly comparable. A net increase in public sector borrowing of this order is extremely small when put against the national income which is now approaching £250 billion. It is so small because measures to stimulate the economy are largely self-financing in terms of the extra activity and revenue they generate. It would be sensible house-keeping to afford it, and there are no significant inflationary consequences. It shows what can be achieved if the Government will only stop digging itself further and further into the mire and instead lift up its eyes to see what prudently can be done. I commend it to the Chancellor for Budget Day.

At my initial meeting in Hillhead seven weeks ago, I said that if we could get a government which would stop doing a lot of foolish things and do a few wise ones, we could begin to turn the tide. I do not claim more than this for the programme outlined here. To renew the vigour of the economy in the longer term will require more profound achievements: a new partnership between management and labour which only a new non-confrontational attitude to politics can bring about, and a new approach to incomes. I believe that a newly-elected Alliance Government could receive the full-hearted co-operation of the British people of the sort which neither of the class-based parties has been able to command at any time since the war. On that basis we might take as our target the reduction of unemployment to 4-5 per cent (1 million to 1¼ million) in the lifetime of a full Parliament. But the programme I have outlined here could be brought in *now* and it would have a quick and dramatic impact on unemployment. Indeed nothing could better illustrate the importance for Scotland of a government of imagination and commitment than the comparison between the prospect we offer of Scotland's unemployment dropping back towards 200,000 over the next two years, and the prospect offered by Mrs Thatcher of unemployment pushing inexorably on towards 350,000 over the same period.

Cambridge Lecture for Keynes' Centenary

On 1 December 1983, a public meeting was held in the Cambridge Guildhall to commemorate the centenary of the birth of John Maynard Keynes. The audience was estimated at about a thousand people and the speakers were Roy Jenkins, John Kenneth Galbraith and Richard Wainwright. The Cambridge Liberal Association organised the event and published a pamphlet of the proceedings under the title John Maynard Keynes: New wisdom for a new age. *I am indebted to the Cambridge Liberal Association for permission to reproduce Roy Jenkins's speech.*

I never knew Keynes. Indeed I do not believe that I ever saw him, unlike, say, Lloyd George, Baldwin or Léon Blum, whom I saw and heard in public but never met in private. If, however, I could nominate two men whom it might have been possible, without the benefit of a time machine, for me to have encountered, I would choose Keynes and Roosevelt.

This is partly but not wholly on account of their fame. And it is not because they were a pair, the one the theorist and the other the exponent. or 'the sorcerer and the sorcerer's apprentice' — but which could possibly be the apprentice? — as is sometimes superficially thought. Roosevelt certainly never read a word of Keynes's main works (although of course some of those around him did), and their one pre-war meeting was not a success. Keynes was disappointed with Roosevelt's hands, a human feature to which he always attached great importance. They were 'firm and fairly strong, but not clever or with finesse'. Roosevelt on the other hand found Keynes too clever, or at any rate too mathematical and abstruse. He referred to him afterwards as 'the gent', not a very obvious term of approval.

So it is not a question of their going automatically together. It is more that of all the near contemporaries about whom I have read a lot and written a little they are the two the physical impact of whose personality I find it most difficult to imagine and for which I would therefore most like to be able to fall back upon direct memory. In the absence of this I must confess that the most vivid 'stills', in the old cinema sense, from Keynes's life have been imprinted upon my mind by Harrod, bowdlerizing though his biography has been shown to be, rather than by Professor Skidelsky. But perhaps that is merely due to the fact that Mr Skidelsky has so far written only about the first part of Keynes's life. And while his life and achievements, being many-sided, can be separated into different strands, they are not in my view very suitable for chopping up into neat little parcels of time.

There are three obvious strands. There is Keynes the semi-(but not very) private man, the Keynes of the Apostles and of the philosophy of G.E. Moore, of Bloomsbury and the South Downs and to some extent the Keynes of Cambridge, the Bursar of King's, the Founder of the Arts Theatre, the bibliophile and picture-buyer, the coruscating conversationalist and controversialist, a man of strong, original and mostly iconoclastic views, an unmatched polemicist. Had this been all, had he negotiated no loans, created no monetary systems and written no word of lasting note, it would still have been enough to make him a figure of continuing, if minor interest. He would have been the twentieth-century equivalent of such nineteenth-century figures as Monckton Milnes, or perhaps Abraham Hayward, who talked so well that, if he were present at dinner, Gladstone, too hurried to wait for the correction of posterity, was said to sulk because he could not compete.

Then there is Keynes the state official, neither a political minister nor exactly a servant of ministers, occupying a position almost without parallel in Britain, but a little more familiar in a French or an American context: a Jean Monnet or a General George Marshall. In this rôle he was adviser, initiator, negotiator, the man of the Paris Peace Conference at thirty-five and of Bretton Woods twenty-five years later, the begetter of Britain's necessary but unpopular post-war American loan. All this would have put him into a substantially higher category of renown. It would have fully justified his Westminster Abbey memorial service, almost unique for an Abbey memorial service for being attended by both his parents. But it would not have made him (with Churchill and more doubtfully Bertrand Russell) one of the two or three most world-famous Englishmen of this century — or perhaps four if Charlie Chaplin is counted as an Englishman. He is put into this category only by his economic writing, and pre-eminently by the *General Theory of Employment, Interest and Money* (1936) which struck such a balance between theoretical elegance and practical application that, being also lucky in its timing, profoundly influenced a generation of world policy-making, extending in its impact to many who, despite the lucidity of his style, never read a single paragraph of his original words. It made him a major station on the line of great economists, which started with Adam Smith, and extends through Ricardo, Mill, and Marshall to himself, but not yet, perhaps never, to any further point of comparable importance.

It is about this aspect of his life, together with his political activities and views, that I have been asked to speak. Professor Galbraith, as I understand it, is to deal with his impact on America and the world. We were both urged to deal with him in a practical and political, rather than an abstract and theoretical, context. That, if I may say so, was an instruction of supererogation, certainly for me but also, if thirty years of warm friendship have taught me anything, for the Professor. It would be rather like asking Talleyrand on one of his rare visits to the seat of his then bishopric at Autun, not to make his sermon too spiritual.

I begin with the politics, and will then turn to the economics. Keynes's Liberalism, it must be said, was not that of a dependable militant. He was a cool Liberal. His first burst of fame came from a denunciation of Lloyd George's policy at the Paris Peace Conference, which was particularly remarkable for the fact that it was a famous polemic with its most polemical passage cut out and only published fourteen years later. However, he was a friend of the Asquiths (more of Margot than of Henry) and infuriated Bloomsbury by saying that he thought that the former Prime Minister was more intelligent than Lytton Strachey. His feeling for Asquith was considerable but was expressed in typical terms which might have commended themselves more to Asquith himself than to some of his more enthusiastic followers. He referred to his quality 'of a certain coolness of temper' which 'seems to me at the same time peculiarly *Liberal* in flavour, and also a much bolder and more desirable and valuable political possession and endowment than sentimental ardours'. Asquith's ardour for Keynes was certainly under control. 'Not much juice to him', he was reported to have said on one occasion. But this may have been after an incident several years earlier when the Prime Minister and Keynes arrived together at Garsington (the scene of the famous Keynes, Strachey, Bertrand Russell photograph) and were announced by the butler as 'Mr Keynes and another gentleman'.

What is more certain is that Keynes, while firmly Asquithian in the days of the Coalition and always more akin, both temperamentally and on grounds of international policy, to Asquith than to Lloyd George, nonetheless moved back into full communion with Lloyd George, on domestic policy at least, under the stimulus of the writing of the Yellow Book and the run-up to the 1929 election. In 1926, just before this period, he came nearest to a precise definition of his political bearings in the Britain of the twenties. He did so with a deadliness of criticism rather than a great gush of enthusiasm:

'How could I bring myself to be a Conservative?' he began. 'They offer me neither food nor drink — neither intellectual nor spiritual consolation. I should not be amused or excited or edified. That which is common to the atmosphere, the mentality, the view of life, of — well, I will not mention names — promotes neither my self-interest nor the public good. It leads nowhere; it satisfies no ideal; it conforms to no intellectual standard; it is not even safe, or calculated to preserve from spoilers that degree of civilization which we have already attained.'

He looked at the Labour Party of those days a shade more charitably but then stated his objection with his habitual eschewal of euphemism:

'Ought I, then, to join the Labour Party? Superficially that is more attractive. But looked at closer, there are great difficulties. To begin with it is a class party and the class is not my class. If I am going to pursue sectional interests at all, I shall pursue my own ... I can be influenced by what seems to me Justice and good sense, but the Class war will find me on the side of the educated bourgeoisie.'

He decided that he was therefore a Liberal, even if by elimination, his main doubt stemming from a lack of confidence in the ability of the Liberal Party, on its own, to regain its pre-war power. He did not want to fight the class war from the other side either. Those who believed 'that the coming struggle was Capitalism versus Socialism and that their duty was to fight Capitalism, ought to get out of the Liberal Party'. He moved on to a still more heartfelt cry: 'I do not wish to live under a Conservative Government for the next twenty years'. The only recipe that he could see as he surveyed the bleak landscape, but one which he propounded without his usual degree of certainty, was Lib-Lab co-operation, with a rejuvenated Liberalism providing most of the ideas.

I think it can be claimed on this evidence, without too much affront to the rule that views on unforeseen events should be only cautiously attributed to the dead, that Keynes would have welcomed the Alliance. Over fifty years ago he wanted to defeat Conservatism, without the Labour Party winning. He saw that the Liberal Party could not do this on its own. It needed a partner. But the only avoidable choice brought one back to the Labour Party, the second of the (for him) unloved ugly sisters. Cinderella had not been created. He would surely have rejoiced in her birth. The Alliance was made for him. I wish he were here to help make it.

The only qualification which must be considered in the interests of the astringent fairness and accuracy which is a characteristic of all (or at least most) Alliance pronouncements is that, like some but not all others, he took a slight lurch to the right in the last years of his life. In 1938 he had supported Cripps' Popular Front campaign, but in October 1939 he wrote to the *New Statesman*, which he had done much to create but which he found an ungracious child:

'The intelligentsia of the Left were loudest in demanding that the Nazi aggression should be resisted at all costs. When it comes to a showdown scarce four weeks have passed before they remember that they are pacifists and write defeatist letters to your columns, leaving the defence of freedom and of civilisation to Colonel Blimp and the Old School Tie for whom Three Cheers.'

The perhaps deliberately odd grammar (rather reminiscent of Queen Victoria's famous 'these news are dreadful' telegram to Gladstone after the fall of Khartoum) suggest that he was writing with emotion, and justifiably so in my view. There would be no conflict with us there. There were, however, a few signs of a retreat from radicalism in his remaining six and a half years. I suppose that one could have imagined him as a Macmillan Tory in the late fifties at the age of seventy-six. But, whatever had happened in the meantime, and even at the age of ninety-six, post-1979 policies would assuredly have brought him coruscatingly back into the anti-Conservative fold. A waste of resources greater even than in the thirties would have been a most powerful twitch upon the thread. The intellectually slipshod nature of the monetarist case, accompanied by the complacent Panglossian belief that there is no alternative, must have aroused his mocking contempt. But above all he would certainly have been repelled by the sheer irrationalism of judging economic policies not by material results but as though it were a religious practice in which the purification of the spirit could be achieved by the mortification of the flesh. There may be some fields of human endeavour in which this is so, but the management of the economy is certainly not one of them.

So much for trying to predict on the basis of Keynes's known but not unchanging views what would have been his developing political orientation. My next task is to try to appraise with the benefit of forty-eight years of hindsight what was the economic and indeed political impact of his main theoretical work.

The General Theory of Employment, Interest and Money was published in January 1936. It did not arrive unheralded, for Keynes had been writing and talking a good deal around the subject of demand deficiency and the under-use of resources in the preceding several years. He had developed at least one of the major ideas — the absence of any causal connection between savings and investment — in *A Treatise on Money* (published in 1930) and he also made substantial use of tools fashioned and announced by others, most notably of R.F. Kahn's 'multiplier', which dates publicly from June 1931. But the *General Theory* was certainly not derivative. Keynes was more open to the charge that he had been too busy to read enough of the works of others. It was an elegant work of theory but it was also urgent, in the sense that it was a direct response to the major economic problem of the time. This accounted for much of its impact.

In addition it was complete, although not perfectly finished, it was new, and it fully justified its title of 'general'. It was complete because it was not just a torpedo fired at the hull of neo-classical economics. Keynes and others had let off a lot of these in the past. But this was a new model ship to set alongside the old. It incorporated some traditional features, and some of the new ones were not wholly watertight. But it was recognisably different, a full-scale re-shaping of the doctrines of macro-economics in terms directly relevant to the major problems of the time.

It was new because previous general theoretical works had assumed that supply created its own demand. The unspoken premise, except in special studies of the trade cycle, was full employment. If it did not exist, it was because wages were too high or some other rigidity had tiresomely but temporarily intervened. The real issue of economics was the most effective allocation of resources, not that they might never be created.

Keynes changed the angle of view. To an excessive extent he regarded the allocation of resources as a resolved issue, and he was prepared to leave the problems of supply to businessmen, which meant that he regarded them as very minor. He was concerned with demand, which, contrary to accepted doctrine, had no natural tendency to settle at full employment level.

The classical theory held that the rate of interest combined with the wage level would perform any necessary corrections. Keynes argued that neither of these mechanisms would work. He dismissed the traditional view of the rate of interest as not merely inadequate but as nonsense. There might well be decisions to save without subsequent decisions to invest. No manipulation of the rate of interest or the money supply alone could deal with this. There would be no increase in the 'propensity to invest' to offset the decreased level of consumption. The economy would simply settle down at a lower level of activity.

A lowering of wages might be equally ineffective as a route to full employment. It was dangerously easy to draw a false analogy between an individual firm and the economy as a whole. (He would no doubt have found Mrs Thatcher's economic equation of a family with a State still more intellectually derisory.) If, with total demand remaining constant, one firm could get its wages down, it would of course tend to employ more people. But in the economy as a whole the decline in total demand was much more likely to cancel out any beneficial employment tendency.

The key was investment. It was the element of demand which fluctuated most and was in the greatest need of stimulus from government. This led Keynes on both to advocating an active rôle for the

State in investment policy ('When the capital development of a country becomes a by-product of the activities of a casino, the job is likely to be ill-done') and to deficit financing in certain circumstances. Balanced budgets when resources were under-used was a mark not of virtue but of stupidity. As a result he became pinned with an inflationary tag. But this was economic primitivism. *How to Pay for the War*, which he published four years later, was written within the assumptions of the *General Theory*, but offered a prescription for war-time finance which, had it been followed by Lyndon Johnson twenty-five years later, might have done more to avoid the great world inflation of the seventies than all the words of Milton Friedman.

What Keynes rejected with contumely was that it was sensible to prescribe the same remedy in totally different circumstances. He had rebutted a charge of inconsistency in 1931: 'I seem to see the elder parrots sitting round and saying: "You can *rely* on us". Every day for thirty years, we have said "What a lovely morning!" But this is a bad bird. He says one thing one day and something else the next.'

Another quality of the *General Theory* was that it endeavoured to re-unify economics. Previously the study of demand and the factors of production had become sharply divorced from the study of banking and monetary policy. As Keynes put it: 'We have all of us become used to finding ourselves sometimes on one side of the moon and sometimes on the other, without knowing what route or journey connects them ...' He provided the connection. It was indeed a general theory.

Keynes did not understate the importance of his book. He wrote to Bernard Shaw a year before publication saying: 'To understand my state of mind ... you have to know that I believe myself to be writing a book on economic theory which will largely revolutionize ... the way the world thinks about economic problems'. 'I can't predict what the final upshot will be in its effect on actions and affairs', he added. 'But there will be a great change, and in particular the Ricardian foundations of Marxism will be knocked away.' This was both a bold and an odd claim. It is not the 'Ricardian foundations of Marxism' which have been the main victim. It is rather the framework of traditional 'capitalist' economics which was first sundered and then put together in another mould. Keynes thought it 'moderately conservative in its implications'. In other words, as Professor Seymour Harris, perhaps his most devoted American exponent of his own generation wrote: 'Keynes's mission ... was to save capitalism not to destroy it'.

A number of his Cambridge peers, including Pigou, his old teacher, and Robertson, his old collaborator, had not greatly liked it. This was partly because he had not gone out of his way to be gracious and had attacked Pigou in typically astringent terms. Pigou, after an interval of ten years and Keynes's death, was notably gracious in return: 'We were pedestrian, perhaps a little complacent . . . Economics and economists came alive. The period of tranquillity was ended. A period of active and . . . creative thought was born. For this the credit was almost wholly due to Keynes'.

So from the academic response to the political effect. There was little significant influence on policy-making in Britain before the War. The position in America is more arguable, but I leave that to Professor Galbraith. What is certain is that the main practical impact throughout the world came after and not before the War. By then Keynes's central doctrine had achieved most powerful practical vindication. The principal economy which was stimulated but not ravaged by war was that of the United States. The increase of national output was there so great that it made possible not only a vast outpouring of war material but a substantial increase in private consumption as well. Munitions production proved a good substitute for his old mocking recipe of getting the Treasury to fill old bottles with bank notes, burying them in disused coal mines and leaving it to private enterprise to dig them up again.

Thereafter there was a quarter century and more with no return, either in the United States or, after post-war recovery took off, in the other principal industrial countries to the massive debilitating unemployment of the inter-war years. There was also in the countries in the European Community and in Japan the greatest surge to wealth that has ever been seen in recorded history. How far this was due to Keynes's writings and their ripple effect is difficult to judge. What is undoubtedly true is that his analytical methods, combined with the greatly improved provision of national income statistics, which he had done a lot to prod along in Britain, affected the whole post-war economic practice and discussion of demand management in the finance ministries and the central banks of the world. No one in 1951 or 1961 or even 1971 (1981 is a different matter) could have spoken in the terms used by Montagu Norman in 1931 and escaped public ridicule. 'Crude Keynesianism', as it has for some time been fashionable to describe some applications of his doctrine, may have some limitations, but it was an immense advance on crude pre-Keynesianism, and is in any event not where Keynes's thought would have stopped had he been alive today.

As in addition he did a great deal to fashion the sun of the Bretton Woods system — although by no means in the exact form that he would have wished — which warmed world trade over the same period, his contribution to this generation-long period of economic success must be regarded by any standards as remarkable and unique.

This success cracked gradually but not evenly over the seventies. First in 1971 the strain of being the pivot of the world monetary system became too great even for the dollar. And it should be said in passing that had Keynes's own Clearing Union scheme prevailed at Bretton Woods the strain would have been more evenly spread and the system might have lasted longer. But it did not so prevail, and the world moved into a disruptive era of violent and often irrational currency fluctuations. Trade and investment both suffered. Then in 1973 came the first wave of oil price increases with its inflationary effect on prices and its deflationary effect on the levels of economic activity in the West. By 1978 some attempt at concerted recovery was under way. But within six months of the Bonn Economic Summit, at which this was planned, the second wave had a still more devastating effect upon both Western and Third World economies, and was fortified by the growth of the doctrine that the way to deal with slump was to make it deeper. As a result we have been back, so far as wasted output and wasted lives, even if not as absolute poverty is concerned, to the conditions of the thirties from which Keynes helped to rescue us. And approximately there, unless new policies are pursued, we show every sign of staying.

How, in view of this history, it can be rationally contended that Keynesianism has been the road to disaster and its monetarist rejection the key to success, I cannot begin to understand.

What, on the contrary, is needed now both nationally and internationally, is an injection into Downing Street, the White House and other chancellories of the world of some of the rational panache which Keynes showed nearly fifty years ago. We may not see his like again, but let us at least hope that the world economy is not ruined by his denigrators.

The World Economy

In December 1982, speaking at the Bridge of Weir, Roy Jenkins set Britain's economic problems in a world context. In January 1983 he delivered a slightly different version of this speech in New York.

It is time to speak out against the policies of deflation and protectionism which have driven the world into the deepest slump for fifty years and threaten to make it still worse.

The Prime Minister's comments on the world economy in her November speech at the Guildhall were among the most depressing to have been uttered by any Western leader, betraying the same narrowness of view, the same lack of imagination, the same absence of hope, with which we in Britain have become all too familiar in relation to our own domestic circumstances. Faced with the most severe depression which any of us can remember, she urged every country, turning inwards, to put its shop in order. 'Countries which have overspent and overborrowed must reduce their spending and reduce their borrowing', she said, and her narrow perception of national interest has convinced her that this country — and indeed the European Community as a whole — should play its full part in the growing slide towards protectionism which threatens to generate a second great wave of recession, with untold consequences as the dominoes making up the world's financial system fall and begin to knock each other down.

Even in terms of narrow national interest, it is short-sighted for a Prime Minister addicted to blaming the economic troubles of this country on the 'world recession' to recommend further deflation of our overseas market. Equally, the leader of a major country which exports a higher proportion of its output than any other should surely see the risks to those exports of a dalliance with protectionism. The interests of the world economy as a whole, and of Britain as part of the world, are the same: to reject deflation and protectionism and to work together for growth and the expansion of world trade.

I believe that this is the moment to propose to our main trading partners that we jointly proclaim a change of course. The world was catapulted into the slump by the two great oil crises, and by the restrictive monetary policies with which governments sought to contain the inflationary consequences. The slump has been made worse by wildly fluctuating exchange rates which have discouraged the growth of investment and trade. It is nonsense to pretend, as Mrs Thatcher does, that these fluctuations reflect reality. They do nothing of the sort. How can they when the yen has been depressed while Japanese exports have been sweeping the world? It is no longer trade patterns which set exchange rates. It is, perversely, exchange rates which set trade patterns. This danger is intensified as a result of the over-extended position many of the private banks have got themselves into in lending to heavily indebted countries. They are now less willing or able to go on lending, and the supply of finance necessary to lubricate the wheels of trade is being withdrawn.

But circumstances are changing, and as they do so the opportunity for effective concerted action emerges. The oil price has stabilised and is unlikely to rise significantly in the foreseeable future. The rate of inflation is falling around the world and interest rates have at least temporarily come down. As world-wide concern about unemployment mounts, circumstances have become propitious for an international initiative to save the world from the disaster which continued adherence to Mrs Thatcher's prescriptions will bring. Opinion is turning in the United States as monetary targets are effectively abandoned. Concern is rising in Germany as unemployment goes over two million even there. We should seize this moment to halt this Gadarene rush towards protection and launch instead a co-ordinated strategy for expansion of the world economy.

To find a way out of the world recession, joint action will be required on three fronts:

First, co-ordinated expansion. If countries are successfully to expand, they must do so together. Otherwise, if one country makes a 'dash for growth' alone, its expansion is likely to be brought to an end by balance of payment difficulties and the inflationary pressures which follow from a collapsing exchange rate. Co-ordinated expansion is far more easily sustainable, and we should give a lead in seeking such an agreement. It *was* achieved at the 1978 Bonn economic summit, in which I took part as President of the European Commission. There, following expansionary moves by both the United States and Britain, Japan in its turn undertook to raise its growth rate by 1.5 per cent. Germany took action to raise its Gross National Product (GNP) by 1 per cent. And France, Italy and Canada all undertook to make contributions of their own.

This exercise was aborted by the second oil crisis, which ushered in the general move towards restrictive policies which carried us all into the great slump. But the rationale remains valid, and my first proposal is that now there should be a major political effort to revive it. Relatively small adjustments to the fiscal stance of the major countries involved could produce significant increases in Gross National Product (GNP) and reductions in unemployment. The world could gradually be led out of recession by imaginative decisions such as Keynes propounded and Roosevelt took. Mrs Thatcher is now the longest serving western leader. Does she wish to follow a Hoover or Roosevelt course? Does she wish to rest upon the peripheral triumph of the Falklands, or does she wish to see Britain leading the world to a solution of its central debilitating problem? Such a solution would mean eating a lot of words, but, as Churchill said, that can be a healthy diet.

Second, monetary stability. Co-ordinated expansion will not succeed unless exchange rates are given a reasonable stability. The economic performance of countries inevitably varies in terms of growth in productivity and comparative inflation. We cannot therefore just proclaim a new regime of fixed exchange rates. The simple re-establishment of the Bretton Woods system of fixed rates is not a practical option today.

Yet there is mounting disillusionment with freely-floating currencies. Experience of these has not been that they adjust gradually and smoothly, keeping payments in balance. On the contrary, exchange rates have lurched wildly from one extreme to another — in the British case from a pound/dollar rate of 1.60 to 2.40 and back again. And not only have they been unstable, but they have shown an ability to stay well out of line — in terms of the requirements of competitiveness — for long periods. The pound is over-valued by thirty to forty per cent compared with its 1975 level and the dollar by thirty per cent, while the yen is at least twelve per cent down. In Britain's case, the result has been to destroy competitiveness and accelerate de-industrialisation.

The markets themselves cannot and do not ensure that currencies adjust to reality so as to keep foreign payments in balance and employment reasonably full. What is required is a system of exchange rates which broadly maintains the competitive position of one economy against another and avoids the short-term fluctuations which are so devastating to investment decisions.

I believe that substantial progress could be made on a trilateral basis between the US, the members of the European Monetary System, which should ever more obviously include Britain, and Japan. Each bloc would define a 'target zone' for its currency within which the value would be free to vary. From time to time the limits of the zones would be shifted upwards or downwards according to medium-term changes in relative competitiveness. Monetary policy would be used to keep the rates within the zones. They should not be permitted to go outside in response to short-term factors. Adequate swap agreements, which are not difficult to secure, can iron out disruptive short-term waves, although they cannot — nor should they — obviate the need for responding to a long-term swell of the ocean.

The new tripod would form the basis of a new and stable (but not rigid) international monetary system, since it would be possible and desirable for other countries strongly dependent on one or other of the blocs to tie their currencies to the Dollar, the Yen or the ECU.

Third, finance for the developing world. The danger of a knock-on collapse of the banking system is now looming. It is not certain. It should not be exaggerated. But it is there. And increased risks mean that private financial lending is being much reduced. If the expansionary strategy outlined above is put into operation, and growth rates raised by an average annual rate of about one per cent as a result, World Bank estimates indicate that large increases in the flows of both official and private finance to developing countries would be needed if general expansion were not to be frustrated by credit constraints. There must at least be a doubling of International Monetary Fund quotas and a fresh issue of Special Drawing Rights — preferably angled in favour of developing countries; there must be a major extension of 'co-financing', which means close co-operation between the official institutions and private banks.

The private banks must have sufficient confidence to continue lending on the scale required. This means help with debt servicing for those developing countries whose total exports barely pay for their interest charges. It means support for the new $20 billion IMF facility for use in cases like the recent one of Mexico. This is not soft-hearted generosity. It is imaginative self-interest for the western world such as was spectacularly shown by the United States at the time of the Marshall Plan which led to the most economically successful years in the recorded history of the world. It also led to the most freely accepted period of American leadership. That cannot be wholly recreated. The balance of the world has changed. Leadership must now come from both sides of the Atlantic, and Britain, if it can achieve self-confidence without chauvinism and discipline without despair, can play a central role.

My first two proposals would provide a context within which expansion could restart — measured, balanced, sustainable expansion —and my third would ensure that it would not run into a barrier of markets blocked by penury. The key phrases are 'stable currencies' and 'a world of good neighbours', starting with those nearest to us, as good neighbourliness must always do. They are the keys which will unlock a gate out of a dark age of deflation and protectionism. They alone once again give us the realistic prospect of restoring jobs, growth and the expansion of trade.

Sterling Buffeted

In a letter to The Times *published on 18 January 1985, Roy Jenkins was sceptical of the handling of sterling by the Prime Minister and the Chancellor.*

Sir, Your Tuesday leader (January 15) was rightly critical of the Government, but for the wrong reasons. The central fault of the extreme monetarist view which the Government embraces, although not enthusiastically enough for you, is its irrationality. It judges policies by valour not by result.

Such anti-empiricism may have its place in certain fields of human endeavour, but not in the management of the economy — or of the exchange rate. These are material processes to be judged by material results.

What actually happens then has to be either ignored or distorted. Lack of confidence in Britain's anti-inflationary prospects is not the reason why the recent strength of the dollar has led to the collapse of sterling, but to a much less severe downward movement in, for example, the French franc.

The primary cause is that the rest of the world cannot see how we are going to pay our way when the oil runs down. Much of our industry was destroyed by the complacent neglect that allowed the pound to soar unrealistically in 1980-1. And that part which remains is still so uncompetitive that even with the pound at a weighted trade index of 71 (against 100 in 1975) we have markedly failed to get our full share of the recent surge of imports into the United States.

What is the point of the Government constantly congratulating itself on the splendid leanness of British industry when most of the evidence is that it is malnutrition and not muscular tone which has been achieved?

Then we have the extraordinary pantomime-horse act of 10 Downing Street and the Treasury over last weekend. If July was a rehearsal of incompetence, January's performance showed that practice makes perfect.

Mr Shore's egregiousness of two years ago, when he proclaimed that the policy of a Labour Government would be a gradual devaluation of thirty per cent, pales into insignificance compared with the Government announcing its indifference to a one-dollar pound and then being annoyed at the market reaction. He was only a *shadow* Chancellor.

A large part of the trouble stems from a combination of the present Chancellor's insensitivity and the Prime Minister's unamiable tendency always to blame something or someone other than herself. As a result, she handles the exchange rate with peculiar ineptitude. It cannot, of course, be commanded by any Government. But it can be considerably influenced by a firm and consistent policy to behave less erratically and more in our national interests.

This is not achieved by treating market forces as though they were junior ministers, first patted on the head as her own special progeny, then sternly ordered to stop behaving independently and improperly, and finally assailed with a flailing mass of misleading statistics.

To suggest, as the Prime Minister did on Tuesday, that the performance of the Deutschmark and the pound are similar is to stretch credulity beyond the limit; and to bewail, as she also did, the fact that no single country has reserves large enough to make an impact on speculation (which is not wholly true) while standing out from achieving the combined *masse de manoeuvre* which could come from membership of the European Monetary System (EMS) is, to say the least, perverse.

The Government's main form of defence is the purely debating one of asking any critic exactly what exchange rate they want. There is no immaculate answer, if only because it is often difficult to move away from a position to which one would not have wished to get in the first place.

What can be said, however, is that we want a rate a good deal more stable than we have seen in the past three-and-a-half years years of plunge from $2.60 to $1.10 and that we want one which is at least partly determined by some rational thought in the Treasury and the Bank of England.

Sterling is no longer in the upper second rank of world currencies as are the yen and the D-Mark but its management is still of great importance to Britain and some considerable importance to the world. The evidence steadily mounts that Mrs Thatcher and Mr Lawson, by performance and temperament, are unfitted to be in charge of such a currency. It is almost impossible to imagine the comment which would have been forthcoming from the Opposition, the City and, not least, you, Sir, had recent *dégringolades* been presided over by anyone other than a Conservative Prime Minister and Chancellor.

Yours faithfully,
ROY JENKINS,
St Amand's House,
East Hendred,
Oxfordshire,
January 17.

Reply to the Budget Speech, 1984

Responding on television to the Chancellor's 1984 budget, Roy Jenkins had the following to say:

Budgets are not nearly as important as Chancellors think they are. Nor are they mostly quite as awful as Shadow Chancellors say they are.

What is obviously important is how the country performs over the year; what's happening to unemployment, to prices, to the standard of living, to the care of the sick and the poor and the old, and to whether we are strengthening or weakening the future of the nation. Budgets do not determine all these things. But they affect them — although often most through missed opportunities. And they provide us with a useful annual occasion to consider whether or not we are on the right national track.

This Budget was very well presented and there are some good things in it, most notably the abolition of the National Insurance Surcharge, because a tax on jobs must be foolish in present circumstances. I believe some of the tax reform measures are sensible, and within a limited framework rather bold, but they do not help small businesses which lose on the swings of capital allowances without gaining on the roundabout of corporation tax. And I greatly regret that child benefit, which is much the most cost effective way of relieving poverty, has not been substantially increased, that the mean cut in housing benefit has not been restored, and that the long-term unemployed who are the most obvious casualties of the Government's strategy are not given the long-term rate of supplementary benefit.

Even more serious are the issues which Mr Lawson with all his tax reforming ingenuity, has simply chosen to ignore. If I were Chancellor now I would be preoccupied with two problems. First, the fact that even after a year or two of pick-up in the economy we still have record levels of unemployment — substantially higher than in almost any competitor country. And there is no prospect on present policies of any significant reduction. Mr Lawson, to be fair to him, did not pretend there was. He just treated the unemployed as something we have to live with, and worth only the most perfunctory of mentions. And that is simply not acceptable.

This year we may well be reaching the top of a little boom. It may be short-lived. The American economy is likely to turn down after their election in November and we may do so with them. To start the next turn down, whenever it comes, with over three million out of work really is a horrifying prospect. Where are we going to finish it? Apart from the hopelessness of the outlook for so many individuals, young and not so young, what is it going to do to the cohesion of our society, to peace on our streets and safety in our homes? In these circumstances I do not think it is enough to have a Chancellor who puts the general direction on automatic pilot and occupies himself, however cleverly, even worthily, with shifting round the seating and the other fixtures.

But it is worse than that. The second problem that dominates my mind is this: how are we going to earn a living when North Sea oil begins to run out? The scale of this problem is vast, but its time scale is now short. Although it is difficult to believe it when one looks around at the industrial wastelands and the generally run-down state of a lot of Britain, we *are* living through a short period when this country for once is peculiarly favoured. None of our competitors has an oil surplus. We have — for the moment a big one. It, and it alone, prevents us being in huge deficit with the rest of the world. In 1983 oil contributed £8 billion in taxation to the Chancellor's revenue. For a year or so it will get bigger still. Then it will begin to go, and it is likely to go with gathering momentum. Within nine years, all the surplus will probably be gone. There will then be a huge gap which will have to be filled with other exports — and they will not come from the dismantled factories or closed down shipyards.

Confronted with this lowering prospect — in many ways the most menacing economically which has confronted us since 1945 — I believe the primary duty of our Government is to use the remaining period of oil spate to put Britain in the best possible shape for a difficult future: to strengthen our real assets: our bridges and railways, ports, water systems, housing stock; the thrust and range of our industry; and our technical skill and training. And such a programme would put a lot of people back to work. We are not doing it at the present time. Unless we do we shall have wasted the window of opportunity presented by the oil. The Chancellor eccentrically claimed on Tuesday that the danger was in bequeathing debt to the next generation. But the real burden of debt today is less than two-thirds of what it was a generation ago. The real danger is bequeathing a run-down Britain without the skills or the tools to earn its living.

That is the charge against the Government's strategy. We can greatly improve matters, although the time is now short. But we will not do so upon the basis of a complacent assumption that we are building on success and thus the future is relatively secure. I do not know which I find less convincing: Mr Lawson and Mrs Thatcher pretending that only in 1979 did we begin to emerge from some sort of dark age of moral decay which embraced not only Labour Governments but the Governments of Mr Heath and Mr Macmillan as well; or Mr Hattersley suggesting that poverty, deprivation and unfairness were as unknown as rain in Camelot until that dreadful date, and that some day he and Mr Kinnock will lead us either backwards or forwards — I am not quite sure which — to an unstained earthly paradise. We cannot afford the political claptrap and we cannot afford industrial confrontation either, which the Labour and Tory parties still do so much to foster.

Dogmatic monetarism is now as discredited as nationalisation. The Alliance wants the Government to launch a major programme of re-equipping Britain. And it wants private business to have the freedom, and to show the initiative to respond to the opportunities that this will create. This is the only way to get the jobs. This is the only way to live with a difficult future, neither head down with fear nor head in the sand with self-deceit, but head up with confidence.

CHAPTER II

Defence

The Labour Party's volte-face on defence was one of the principal causes of Labour Party members defecting. The May 1979 Election Manifesto of the Labour Party was resolute in its support of NATO; its acceptance of the need for the British nuclear deterrent within the NATO framework; and its rejection of unilateral nuclear disarmament.

It was one of the great triumphs for the left wing of the Labour Party that, in the atmosphere of post-electoral defeat, the Conferences of 1979, and 1980 brought the Labour Party to a constitutionally binding position on defence that was in complete contrast with what had gone before. The breaking point for many 'exitists' to the SDP was a point-blank refusal to campaign for a Labour Party committed to unilateral disarmament and the expulsion of American manned NATO bases within the United Kingdom. Long years of loyalty to Labour through thick and thin could not withstand the realisation of what such policies would mean to the integrity of the defence of national democratic institutions.

It was a cornerstone of SDP Defence policy to continue to maintain what had been the general theme of the pre-1979 Labour Party: a robust defence force at every level whilst seeking arms reduction by negotiation.

Although many of his by-election and other speeches presented this view of defence policy, Roy Jenkins' first major speech exclusively devoted to the subject was early in 1983 at the Royal Institute of International Affairs in London.

Lecture at Chatham House, 8 February 1983

When I last spoke at Chatham House, twenty-six months ago, the persistent, even if occasionally shaky consensus on long-term British foreign and defence policy had just been sundered in two major ways. The Labour Party, then the only alternative Government, had reversed the position of previous Labour governments on Europe and on unilateralism. It had committed itself to withdrawal from the Community and to the abandonment both of the independent deterrent and of our willingness to provide facilities for an American deterrent.

In these circumstances the fact that it was prepared to remain in NATO amounted to no more than a fig leaf of hypocrisy. A non-nuclear NATO could provide no security against the Soviet Union. Indeed it could not even exist, for the United States manifestly would not keep its troops in Europe if they were required to be bereft of any nuclear protection. Equally a position in which America was graciously allowed to protect Europe with its own deterrent, but in which its principal European partners unctuously washed their hands of any defiling responsibility for its deployment would quickly become unviable. Denmark can half contract out. But Britain, in my view, cannot. So NATO would be effectively destroyed by the then new but continuing Labour Party commitment.

Nonetheless, attention was probably more concentrated upon the European than upon the unilateralist decision. And it was that which, on the occasion of my previous visit, I endeavoured to refute. For one thing, the decision to withdraw from Europe appeared to be running with the grain of popular opinion. The unilateralist decision, on the basis of previous experience, appeared to be running strongly against it. The nuclear issue was not in the forefront of the public mind, but when it had last been so, in the late fifties and early sixties, the great majority, even on Labour voters, had been strongly for a tough stance. The issue had been an internal one, within the left, with few votes to be won by what was then the anti-Gaitskell position.

Curiously something very near to the reverse has proved to be the case. The anti-European current, although apparently wide, has proved also to be shallow. In the two by-elections I have fought, my views on Europe were little of a disadvantage in Warrington and a mild plus in Hillhead. In my view most people have come to a reluctant acceptance that coming out of Europe would disrupt our export trade and destroy yet more jobs. This mood is not a firm foundation for a positive British role in the Community, but it is enough to make the issue an encumbrance for the Labour Party rather than a sharp sword of effective attack. If in Government, they might well try to fudge withdrawal.

The nuclear issue, on the contrary, has dramatically escalated, and, while there are some conflicting currents, not in a way that makes a unilateralist party a clear electoral liability. There is of course much more to be said about it than that. It affects not only our whole future security and defence policy, but also the survival of civilisation.

With such vast stakes involved the form of the debate has been and is profoundly unsatisfactory. For long periods it goes almost completely underground, and is followed only by two minorities: one of committed campaigners, the other of arms control specialists, who mostly embed themselves in jargon and acronyms which make even the multilateral trade negotiations seem a pellucid field of pure English.

Then, when the debate suddenly surfaces, it mostly does so on the issue of a particular weapon, which assumes an excessive importance, and with little regard to its relationship to the whole. A year ago, when I was deeply engaged in the streets and meeting halls of Glasgow, hardly anything was discussed except Trident. Today it is all about Cruise. Such indeed is this concentration and our insularity that there is little mention of Pershing II, because it is not to be here, despite the fact that the repercussions of its deployment would probably be greater than those of Cruise.

I therefore think it desirable to try to look at the matter more in terms of rather simple first principles than is often done:

First, I believe that nuclear weapons do deter, and that there is at least a strong possibility that without them we would not have had peace on the central front — that is in Europe — for the past thirty-eight years. And, given the deadliness of modern conventional weapons, that war would have been still more devastating to lives and the framework of lives than either 1914-18 or 1939-45.

Second, on the other hand, it is powerfully argued that the mounting scale of nuclear weaponry has been such that the risks for the future outweigh the benefits of the stability that has been maintained. Peace may have been aided, but at the price of creating engines of destruction which, if used, would not merely create greater devastation than in any previous war, but could well end civilisation. We move on to a totally different scale of measurement. If we had a retrospective choice, I think we should therefore wish that the Manhattan project had not succeeded, provided, and it is a big proviso, that the German project had not done so either.

Third, however, as we never have retrospective choice, the point is clearly academic. Nothing now is going to remove such weapons from the grasp of mankind. And the ability to create them will be in the hands of an increasing proportion of the nations of the world.

Fourth, but that is not an excuse for fatalism. For at least some time ahead it is only an exchange between the major powers which could destroy civilisation as opposed to creating appalling local destruction. We should not therefore be diverted by thoughts of what Pakistan or Israel could or might do in taking our eyes off the central issue, the East/West balance of terror, and the dangers of such a central conflict. Here at least there is one source of potential comfort. The knowledge of the scale of risk is deeply imbued in Washington and Moscow, as indeed in London and Paris.

Fifth, given that we have to live with the possession at some level of such weapons, it is to me clear that Western unilateralism would make matters worse and not better. The absence of a powerful and totally secure

Western second strike capacity would diminish our chance of safety, let alone that of freedom.

Sixth, nor do I think that a British unilateralism would help. Leaving aside for the moment — I will return to it later — its effect on Atlantic relations, it stems, paradoxically, from a gross under-estimate of the scale of the danger. There is no safety in contracting out. Nor can I accept the view that we would convert by example. There is not a shred of evidence of this.

Seventh, there are, however, several countervailing but not contradictory points which must be made. There can be no victory in a nuclear war. To live with the illusion that there could be is not only to show a singular capacity for unimaginative self-deception but also clearly to overstep any bounds of morality. I hesitate to step into the argument which this week is engaging so many distinguished clerics. But to see deterrence is the best hope of preserving peace appears to me to be morally acceptable, whereas to contemplate a strategy of victory through annihilation does not.

Eighth, it follows from this that there is no purpose and considerable danger in seeking nuclear superiority. The ability to destroy the enemy a hundred rather than thirty or even ten times over does not increase security. The net result is a distortion of the balance of NATO military effort, and the relentless but pointless heightening of menace. Nuclear weapons can deter, but not only can they bring no victory, they cannot effectively defend.

Ninth, nor do I find any force in the argument that, even if the West could not win a nuclear military victory over the Soviet Union, it could at least win a nuclear arms race by outpacing them through economic superiority and forcing them to limp off in the field, hobbled by bankruptcy. It is a terrifying form of Russian roulette, a game at which the Russians might be expected to be at least as good as we are. Next, national bankruptcy does not actually happen, and certainly not to a super-power. Furthermore, the capacity of Soviet society to divert resources from civilian consumption to military purposes is almost certainly greater than that of American society. And, last, it is by no means obvious that an impoverished Russia would be easier to deal with than a moderately prosperous one.

Tenth, there is therefore a great deal to be said for a freeze of strategic nuclear weapons. And it is in strategic weapon terms that the American protagonists of such a course naturally and primarily think. There is, however, one proviso. A freeze would be much better than an escalation but much worse than a reduction. The best must not be the enemy of the good, but nor should the good be the enemy of the better. On either hypothesis British Trident looks increasingly objectionable. The idea that we could increase the number of our nuclear warheads, transported by a most powerful means of delivery, by five or six times, and expect it either not to be counted in the East/West balance or to be regarded as a contribution to arms control is nonsense.

Eleventh, the 'theatre' or intermediate-range nuclear missile position is more complicated. The present arrangements for the deployment of Cruise and Pershing II are closely interlocked not only with the success or failure of the Intermediate-range Nuclear Forces (INF) talks but also with US/European relations. However much one may disagree with aspects of the Reagan Administration's nuclear assumptions, the North Atlantic Alliance must transcend such a disagreement with one Presidency or for that matter one Prime Ministership, for Mrs Thatcher appears to endorse most of the fallacies of President Reagan and Secretary Weinberger.

Twelfth, it is also the case that there is a danger of some legitimate American impatience with fluctuating European criticisms. President Carter was criticised by some European leaders for not making up his mind to deploy the neutron bomb. President Reagan was criticised by some European leaders for making up his mind to do so. Equally the 'dual track' policy on Cruise and Pershing II was evolved following a European initiative. Now this essentially political decision has raised a hornets' nest of European opposition and hesitation. It is understandable, for Europe is torn between a fear that America will desert us and an apprehension that she wants to use us as, for her, a relatively safe battleground. We must be careful of trying to have it both ways.

Thirteenth, there is also the vital and immediate question of our negotiating position vis-à-vis the Russians in the Intermediate-range Nuclear Forces. I think that the Russians may want to do a mutually acceptable deal. We cannot be certain. There is obviously a substantial element of propaganda in Mr Andropov's offers. But so there is in President Reagan's zero option. One thing, however, is as near to certain as anything can be in this arcane field. The Russian leadership will sometimes give something for something. They will never give something for nothing. I would therefore not be in favour of a freeze on today's position for intermediate-range missiles. To do so would be damaging both to transatlantic confidence and to our negotiating position in INF.

Fourteenth, therefore, to sum up, I would say no to unilateralism, no to foolish and dangerous assumptions about the possibilities of nuclear victory or nuclear superiority, no to Trident, a freeze on strategic weapons if better cannot be obtained, but continuing with the Cruise and Pershing deployment plans — whilst still hoping they may not be necessary — in the interests both of getting a deal with the Russians and of not rocking Atlantic unity by an inconsistency of European purpose. The double safety catch is desirable. So is a battlefield nuclear-free zone. If Mr Andropov wants it wider than the Palme Commission suggested, then that can certainly be examined. So, equally clearly, is a strengthening of Western conventional forces. A raising of the nuclear threshold must be right, even if one remains a little sceptical of the dramatic effect of a three per cent per annum increase in real expenditure.

All of this underlines the need for a greater internationalist commitment by Britain. We cannot contract out of the nuclear threat, but we can do a good deal in co-operation to help reduce it. In the European Community we cannot solve the British budgetary problem by standing half off-shore. We could significantly mitigate our unemployment problem by sensible measures at home, but we certainly cannot hope to cure it except as part of concerted action on expansion, currency stability, and greater flows of finance to the Third World. Our weakness is that we alternate between supineness and bursts of independent action or desire for independence. There is a chauvinism both of the right and the left. We have not solved our problems by the martial valour of the Falklands expedition, nor will we solve them by getting rid of American bases. We have still not come to terms with our position as a medium-grade power. Until we do, British influence will be less than it could be.

NATO Article for *The Times*

1984 marked the thirty-fifth anniversary of NATO and Roy Jenkins was invited by The Times *to contribute an article in a series on the subject. As with the European Community, the other great institution founded by leaders of courage and foresight, Roy Jenkins's theme in discussing NATO was to urge a revival of the energy that was put into its creation.*

The North Atlantic Treaty was signed by twelve members in Washington on 4 April 1949. Only seven of them had been involved in the detailed negotiations. It had all been put together in a period of just over a year. It would have been a most formidable feat of political engineering in any event. As the period was bisected by a most keenly fought presidential election, which the incumbent was expected to lose, in the country which had to make overwhelmingly the greatest contribution in terms both of resources and of sacrifice of tradition, it becomes simply prodigious.

It makes the present habit of the ten member governments of the European Community of grinding through council after council, turning them each into an accountants' wrangle but reaching no solution even to the accountancy problem, let alone embracing wider issues, seem not merely puny but a disgraceful abdication of leadership. Sir Geoffrey Howe, as Mrs Thatcher claims, may be a 'brilliant negotiator' in this forum but it is an impasse and not a constructive solution which is too often the outcome of his, her, and everyone else's current negotiations.

Contrary to the 'revisionist' view that the Americans encouraged the cold war to enable them to create NATO, and thereby dominate Western Europe, they were distinctly hesitant in the early stages. Nor did the French help much. They were in favour — Gaullist detachment came later — but thought principally in terms of the maximum immediate shipment of American military supplies to France rather than in wider or longer terms.

The Federal Republic did not exist, so there could be no question of West Germany being admitted at that stage. Even the admission of Italy was a matter of considerable controversy until towards the end, but more on the ground of its geographical position than because of ex-enemy status. Norway, Denmark, Iceland and Portugal (in ascending order of exclusion) played little or no part in the negotiations.

Those who were crucial to pushing the United States forward were Britain, Canada and the Benelux countries. The Canadians were much to the fore. It was not merely the preponderance of US power which made it a North Atlantic Treaty. This British and Canadian role may have helped to fuel Bevin's deeply mistaken later suspicions of the purely European Coal and Steel Community.

The still more crucial attribute of the new organisation was however the preponderance within it of American power. In the late 1940s, it was overwhelming: militarily, politically, economically, monetarily. The mainland of western Europe had a great history, and maybe a future, but in the then present it was only just beginning to crawl up from a pit of poverty and near-despair, and escape from being a strategic vacuum. Britain was different. We were the simulacrum of a great power, one of the victorious Big Three. But our resources were grossly over-stretched, and in reality our economy was almost as weak as that of France or Germany or Italy, without having the advantage of being so stripped down as to give us the opportunity to start again.

What was the history of the Alliance over its first decades? First, it contained the Soviet thrust to western Europe. The position never again looked as menacing as it did in 1947-8, with the Communist parties in France and Italy almost poised for a takeover and Berlin beleaguered. Second, it maintained the peace on the central front where the armies and influence of the super-powers were in immediate juxtaposition.

Third, American leadership maintained the broad loyalty of the other members, in spite of the strains of Suez and Dulles's brinkmanship in the

1950s, the US disaster in Vietnam in the late 1960s and early 1970s, and then, partly as a consequence, the collapse of the dollar-centred Bretton Woods monetary system and the partial collapse of the dollar itself.

Fourth, and fairly steadily, there also proceeded an eastwards shift in the balance of power within the Alliance. In every sphere, except that of nuclear strike-power, which itself became less important (but not less dangerous) as the Soviet Union moved towards a position of equality, Europe became both relatively and absolutely stronger, and the US relatively weaker.

That phase now looks to be over. Already, to take the last point first, the combined national income of the Community countries has fallen back to ninety-three per cent of that of the United States. Short-term the gap is widening daily, but the longer-term prospect is much more serious, with Europe dropping behind in the technology of the new industrial revolution to such an extent as to take it out of the league of the US and Japan.

At the same time the political cohesion of the Community is being increasingly lost as the budgetary rows endlessly dominate the available time in the meetings of heads of government and foreign ministers. The much talked of strengthening of the European pillar of the Alliance is not merely not happening; such strength as the pillar had already achieved is being eroded.

Atlanticists who were cool on Europe might argue that this did not matter if it coincided with a prospect of Washington resuming its old effortless captaincy, and this being again freely accepted throughout the West. This is almost the reverse of the reality. 'Effortless' in some senses the leadership of the White House may currently be, but it creates more conflict and suspicion in most of the other members of NATO than at almost any other time in the past thirty-five years.

This contains great dangers. For the foreseeable future the Atlantic Alliance remains as necessary as when it was created. The greatest threats to the peace and indeed the survival of the world arise out of a paradox. On the one hand there is the menace of an unimaginative belief that all that is necessary to learn the lessons of the 1930s — rearm, do not appease, try to out-missile the enemy — and the world will be safe. But on the other hand there is a great need for a steadiness of hand. An inconsistency of purpose could be fatal. The delicacy of the nuclear balance requires predictability on both sides.

If we are to avoid an unnecessary and damaging destabilization of the world, a little more of the spirit of 1949 is necessary across the Atlantic as well as in Europe.

Speech to the Council for Social Democracy

On 15 January 1984 Roy Jenkins addressed the Council for Social Democracy meeting in the University of Aston in Birmingham. On behalf of the platform, he was answering a high-quality Defence debate characteristic of Social Democrats in Council. It was both a major speech and a short speech - he spoke for exactly fifteen minutes.

It expressed the essence of Social Democratic attitudes to Defence policy, a part of the very marrow of the Social Democratic bone.

I have not previously spoken to the Council, except in passing, about defence policy. And because this is the first occasion, I propose briefly to start with some first principles. And to try to explain from these why, in my view, the motion of the Policy Committee, subject to some proposed clarifying and complementary but not contradictory additions, which we shall be happy to accept, represents the most sensible policy for this party and the best contribution which we can make to the peace of the world.

There are two paradoxes of which we must be conscious without being confused. First the unilateralists are right in drawing attention to the scale of the menace. It is of a totally different order from anything we have ever known in recorded history. A major nuclear exchange could certainly destroy civilisation. It might even effectively destroy life on the planet. If unilateralism, protest, the peace movement, the Greenham Common women, were the answer to this, they would be overwhelmingly justified. But the fact that the scale of the danger is such makes unilateralism a response which, while understandable, is wholly inappropriate.

It is not a particular area round a base, not even an individual country, which is at risk if things go wrong. It is the whole world, certainly the whole European/North American populated belt. To proclaim a local nuclear free zone and to believe that this gives safety is to erect a bamboo fence against a hurricane. Fortunately in some ways, the area of risk includes the main population centres of the super-powers, and they know it perfectly well.

In these circumstances the only route to safety is the multilateral route. The other is not merely unwise or hazardous. It is meaningless. It does not deal with the problem. It is as foolish to believe you can find safety by contracting out as it is to be indifferent to the fact that there are now nuclear arsenals on either side of approximately one million times the power of all the bombs dropped in 1945.

The second paradox is that what is required in these circumstances is a mixture of imaginative flexibility and steadiness of hand and purpose. To believe that just to learn the lessons of the thirties — rearm, do not appease — or even those of the great Gaitskellite controversy of 1960 is to be dangerously atrophied in a totally different past. The stakes have become quite different. Yet an inconsistency of purpose could be fatal. The delicacy of the nuclear balance requires predictability on both sides. The worst dangers would arise from a break-up of NATO, which might well encourage Russian foolishness, or, as in a sense I regret to say, a sudden disintegration of the Russian eastern European empire which, particularly if it coincided with a dispute between the military and the party in Moscow, could turn the Soviet Union into a lurching giant.

The latter we can do little about, except to encourage Russian confidence rather than to believe that abusive 'megaphone diplomacy' helps. The former is something to which this country, with West Germany, is nodal. American actions, and still more, American talk, sometimes rightly arouse distrust and disapproval. But let us be in no doubt at all that we still need the Alliance, and that need transcends our view of a particular President — or for that matter a particular Prime Minister.

Let us not deceive ourselves either that the Europeans as a whole are in particularly high standing in Washington at the moment. We are seen as disorganised and vacillating. President Carter's administration was criticised for one set of faults, President Reagan's for the reverse. And there is a dangerous dichotomy in a lot of European feeling about America. We are torn between a fear that she will desert us and an apprehension that she want to use us as, for her, a relatively safe battleground. Let us have the imagination to see how aggravatingly contradictory this can look from the other side of the Atlantic.

Our British interest, indeed the interest of world peace, is in getting arms control agreements not between the Russians and ourselves — that is not very relevant — but between the Russians and the Western Alliance as a whole. We must therefore do nothing to undermine the NATO decision-making machinery, because we need more and not less collective will in the Alliance. That rules out any gimmicky solution like packing up the missiles which have arrived and temporarily sending them back again. A pause, yes. But a reversal without an approach to an agreement, no. That would just be a recipe for chaos in the Alliance.

We must also get the European political voice much more effectively together. It was a disgrace that, at a time of great East/West tension and considerable strains across the Atlantic, the Athens summit, almost without precedent amongst European Councils, could find practically no time for political discussion. Its head was too deep in the groceries.

The basic fact does however remain that the West and the Russians must get back to the negotiating table, and with a greater will to succeed than previously. Nuclear weapons can deter. That is why we must have a totally secure second strike capacity. For this not to be so would increase the risk not merely to freedom but to peace. But they cannot defend and still less could they give victory. The idea of going for victory in a nuclear weapons race is therefore as foolish as it is dangerous. No-one's security is added to by being able to destroy the enemy not fifty but a hundred times over.

And the most threatening weapons undoubtedly increase the risk of stumbling into destruction. I believe that our strategy must be firmly and quickly directed towards 'no first use'. In practice it is, I believe, already so, dictated by the commonsense of self-preservation. But to proclaim it with confidence we must have regard to our conventional defensive capacity.

This is the last debate of the weekend, but it is the biggest issue. We cannot dispose by resolution of what happens. But let us give an example which will be almost unique for a party in opposition, of setting out policy with exactly the same responsibility that we would show if we were in office.

This is far too menacing an issue for the easy slogan and the propaganda trick. It requires an approach of rational internationalism, a quality which is too scarce in British politics, but which I believe is absolutely fundamental to the purposes of this Party. We are as opposed to the weak isolationism of the Left as we are to the jingo isolationism of the Right. We believe that we can only safeguard Britain by safeguarding the world.

The Falkland Islands War

On 2 April 1982 Argentinian troops invaded the Falkland Islands and the small force of British Royal Marines garrisoned there was forced to surrender. Whether the shock was as profound as the Government pretended is a matter that will long exercise commentators on such matters. It may take many years, like with the Suez debacle of 1956, for the full story to emerge. Unlike Suez, however, the result was a complete military victory, a great patriotic revival and the incumbent Prime Minister, Margaret Thatcher, went forward to a successful general election and a second term at 10 Downing Street.

In military terms it was a superbly professional performance from each arm of the services represented there. In terms of international prestige, it demonstrated, as it was meant to do, that Britain would defend its own. There would no longer be doubts about that. In party political terms Mrs Thatcher, who in 1981/2 had been suffering the worst polling results of any Prime Minister since polls were taken, had, by the end of 1982, surpassed every previous Prime Minister except for Winston Churchill in the Second World War.

But it was necessary to think beyond the event itself to the casus belli *and the political solution that must follow the military event.*

On 4 June, eleven days before British troops entered Port Stanley, Roy Jenkins wrote an article for The Times.

The task force has performed with brilliant precision and a complete victory now seems highly likely. While we may reflect on how many lives could have been saved by effective preventive action, it is also appropriate to give thanks for the avoidance of the devastating blow to national morale which would have been involved in a military debacle.

Despite the military triumph, the most difficult problems lie ahead. How we respond to these will provide the test of statesmanship. I am disturbed by the attitude of those, including apparently some members of the Government, who appear to believe that once the Union Jack flies again over the Governor's house in Port Stanley, we can ignore Argentina and such repercussions as there are on the rest of Latin America; and that everything will go on much as before except that, in sharp contrast with 1980, we will assert that British sovereignty is permanently non-negotiable.

This argument is fortified in the minds of some by the fact that brave British men have died in and around the Falklands. This is perhaps an understandable but most dangerous argument. If the loss of blood in battle were to be held to inhibit all subsequent judgement and flexibility, British valour would become the enemy of British interest. We would still be fighting to try to hold India, if not Massachusetts, and all British casualties would be dedicated to setting 'the past upon its throne again'.

Of course the rights of self-determination operate the other way in the Falklands. But we have not been fighting for 'paramountcy'. That was pushed by David Steel out of even Mrs Thatcher's vocabulary. We have been fighting primarily for the rule of law in international affairs, and that is a very fine concept, as it is in domestic affairs. Provided this is upheld it is no service to the dead to insist on a settlement which takes account neither of realities in the South Atlantic, nor of the limits of British military force.

There are, I think, three central reasons why a negotiated settlement is essential after our victory.

First, there is the military problem. Even when Port Stanley airport is improved, and we are thus given the capacity to reinforce our garrison with speed, we would, without a satisfactory settlement, be obliged to retain a substantial military presence to defend the islands. If there were a continuing threat of Argentinian hit and run raids, we would require a formidable force, permanently stationed on the islands, together with significant supporting naval and air units.

Such a force will clearly be required for a time after the retaking of Port Stanley. But it is suggested that we should maintain such a garrison for the next decade and more, with the recurring risk that any new regime in Buenos Aires may decide on a course of increased military confrontation. Our army is already seriously overstretched with its commitments to NATO and in Northern Ireland. Unless we are prepared to make a permanent addition to its strength, a major long-term commitment in the Falklands would be irresponsible.

Quite apart from the effects of such a commitment of our defence policy as a whole (including the types of ships and aircraft that we require), the public expenditure consequences of such a policy would be considerable. This is not a matter that can be swept aside as being of no account. For a government which decided to withdraw HMS *Endeavour* from the South Atlantic, an announcement that may well have persuaded General Galtieri that we were no longer serious about the Falklands, now to take such a view would be profoundly ironic.

Second, we have to consider world opinion and particularly that of the United States. We have received remarkable support from our friends in the European Community, several members of the Commonwealth, and above all in a painfully difficult situation for them, from the United States. It would be wrong to imagine that this support would be retained if we appeared to resist adamantly any sensible long-term solution to the Falklands issue.

The interest of the United States has been damaged by the war. By supporting Britain, it has jeopardized its relations both with Argentina, where it is now at least as cordially disliked as is Britain, and with a great deal of the rest of South and Central America, even among nations that refused to support the Argentine invasion. The United States fears that a prolongation of a military confrontation between Argentina and Britain will increase the likelihood of Soviet and Cuban penetration in the continent.

It would be pointless for us to resent the anxiety of the Americans; to them, Latin America is a vital national interest in a way that no British government, including the present one, has ever regarded the future of the Falklands. Equally it would be foolish to imagine that our other supporters in the world will be eager to agree to long-term sanctions against Argentina. They, too, will expect us to make a sustained attempt after victory to secure a settlement.

Third, there is the folly of imagining that without such a settlement there is any prospect of ending the economic stagnation of the Falklands. Young people will continue to leave, and the Islands will become increasingly isolated from the mainland. They will become even more dependant on Whitehall; without government guarantees there will be negligible inward private investment, and little prospect of any enterprising development of material resources. It is to the British, the victors, and not the vanquished, that world opinion will look for a route out of this impasse. Victory is much sweeter than defeat but it carries more obligations with it.

Almost certainly the best prospect of success in the medium term lies in some form of United Nations trusteeship in which proper account would be taken of the opinions of the islanders; and Argentina would have to be involved in such an arrangement.

It seems fairly clear that Mr Pym would favour an approach along these lines, and I hope that, despite the suggestions now being made by some of her friends, Mrs Thatcher will reconcile herself to it.

She possesses exceptional qualities of determination and courage which I have in the past seen deployed to the advantage of our country. The reverse side of this coin is that she can equate flexibility with moral cowardice and display an insensitive self-righteousness when dealing with colleagues and, still more dangerous, with other heads of government who do not share her own certainties.

It is, however, deeply disturbing that we have now witnessed the second press campaign directed at Mr Pym in his brief period as Foreign Secretary. 'Vilification' was a strong word for a *Times* headline to employ. Earlier this year it was Mr Whitelaw, the Home Secretary, who was subjected to the same treatment. Last year it was Mr Prior, then Employment Secretary. The criticism of Mr Pym is particularly misplaced. As Foreign Secretary he has to deal with the reality of the outside world. His critics do not.

The fact is that we cannot guarantee both the long-term military security and the economic viability of the Falklands. To pretend that this is possible would be dangerous self-deception.

We have, over the past twenty-five years, suffered from two apparently contradictory national faults. One has been a lack of national self-confidence. The other has been an illusory, even a romantic view of our world power. America had to face this battle between conflicting forces after Vietnam. Probably, if we knew more, the Russians did after the Cuban missile crisis.

The great economies built out of defeat, Japan and West Germany, have tried to resolve it by not seeking a political role commensurate with their economic power. France, neither romantic nor humble, has been more successful perhaps at keeping together the two circus horses of aspiration and reality than any other nation.

The Falklands crisis gives us the opportunity to produce a new synthesis. I am profoundly sceptical of the view that it amounts to a national regeneration comparable with 1940. That shows a pathetic lack of proportion. But we have carried through a limited operation extremely well. That ought to help us not to reach beyond our grasp. We have assuaged our honour. Let us now show foresight in victory.

CHAPTER III

The Death Penalty

Speech in the House of Commons, 1982

To be a generalist is in the nature of a Parliamentarian's work. Few Members of Parliament, however, had better specialist experience to offer than Roy Jenkins when he spoke to the House of Commons in the debate on the Criminal Justice Bill on 11 May 1982. Twice Home Secretary, he was first appointed to that post in 1965, a few months after the death penalty had been abolished for a trial period. Roy Jenkins had himself been campaigning for ten years for that abolition. It was not surprising, therefore, that he took a major part in the debate on 11 May 1982; it was also his first debate as a Social Democrat MP, shortly after his by-election success at Hillhead.

A year later, in 1983 (see pages 128-32), speaking on a Private Member's motion on the same subject, Roy Jenkins again delivered an intellectually rigorous speech, and in doing so he crossed swords with Leon Brittan, the new Conservative Home Secretary. Both reports are taken from Hansard.

I have two reasons for wishing to speak in the debate. First, I have the most recent direct contact with the electorate — fairly intensive contact in two by-elections in the past year — and I know that there is concern about this matter, although in neither case was the electorate in any doubt about my views. Secondly, for two separate periods, I held the office of Home Secretary and had to discharge the heavy responsibilities involved in these matters.

Those experiences certainly do not leave me in any mood for dogma on this and other issues. There are many questions relating to crime and punishment to which none of us knows the answer and we mislead ourselves and the public if we pretend too much that we do. There are great dangers, as perhaps the Government and the Prime Minister found after the last election, in trying to make this a party issue. (Hon. Members: 'She did not'.) The right hon. Lady did. I was interested that eventually, in February or March, she agreed with the right hon. Member for Cardiff, South-East (Mr Callaghan) that it did not make much difference who was Prime Minister when dealing with these difficult problems.

No one can fail to be impressed by and to take seriously the deep sense of concern about violent crime and the fear that it provokes which is now in the minds of many people, particularly, although not exclusively, the old. It would be quite wrong for any of us to pretend that the forces of enlightenment are entirely on one side in this matter or to try to dismiss as a mere desire for atavistic vengeance the feelings of those who search for some protection that they believe would make them feel more secure.

Therefore, in considering this matter, I have tried to set aside what I regard as the traditional arguments against the death penalty — those which certainly persuaded me and were deployed with great force in the debates leading up to the 1965 decision. I have always regarded the, in some ways corrupting and certainly macabre, ritual of the death penalty as repugnant, but I believe that it is one's duty to set aside those feelings if I was persuaded that the death penalty would help to give security and protection to people who feel great need for security and protection at this time.

Having said that, I am not so persuaded, for three reasons which I shall try to state briefly.

First, the worst form of mass murder and mutilation that we have experienced recently has without question resulted from terrorist acts on a mass scale. The hon. Member for Ilford, North referred to 1974. In that year twenty-one young people were killed in a pub bombing incident in Birmingham. At that time, I was Home Secretary and I represented a Birmingham constituency. It was my duty to visit in hospital not those who had been killed, but the many who had been mutilated not just in that incident but in four or five others. What is involved is, therefore, deeply engraved on my mind. I have been as close to it as any hon. Member, with perhaps a few exceptions, such as the right hon. Members for Stafford and Stone (Sir H. Fraser) and Sidcup (Mr Heath) who have experienced direct attacks.

As the hon. Member for Ilford, North made clear, terrorism is a major threat. On the face of it, it would be curious to suggest that we should have the death penalty for some forms of murder, but exclude it for terrorism. It is what I believe some hon. Members may have in mind. I do not believe that it can begin to be convincingly argued that capital punishment for terrorism would be either wise or protective.

First, is the death penalty to be used in Northern Ireland or only in Great Britain? I remember the right hon. member for Leeds, North-East (Sir K. Joseph), now Secretary of State for Education and Science, announcing his conversion to using it in Great Britain, but saying that it must be excluded from Northern Ireland. It seemed to me a most extraordinary proposition. One comes forward with what is said to be a unique and effective deterrent, but where the threat is greatest the sword is left in its sheath and it is drawn only where the threat is less. I find that a difficult proposition to accept. Yet everyone who has been directly concerned with security and the administration of the law in the horribly difficult circumstances of Northern Ireland knows that the death penalty would make things worse, not better.

The most knowledgeable convert is the Home Secretary himself who, of course, abolished capital punishment in Northern Ireland in 1972. The right hon. Gentleman has certainly learned from his experience. Apart from anything else, it would make it impossible to continue with the Diplock courts. Could anyone seriously argue that we could have the supreme penalty without trial by jury in one part of the United Kingdom?

Mr W.R. Rees-Davies (Thanet, West): Perhaps the right hon. Gentleman will consider this point. I do not know whether he considered it when he was Home Secretary. If the treason law is applied, where the death penalty exists anyway and it becomes recognised that acts of terrorism create the offence of treason felony because every one of the persons concerned commits treason against the State, that might make it unnecessary to amend the terrorism new clause. Why has that law not been brought into effect? Surely, if the law needs to be amended, it can be done in that way. That would take into account the large number of IRA murders that have been perpetrated.

Mr Jenkins: I do not understand the point of the hon. and learned Gentleman's argument. I am concerned with the substance, not the legal form. I am concerned with whether hanging, or any other form of judicial killing, for terrorist crimes would give greater or lesser security to the innocent.

My point was whether one could possibly use the supreme penalty —even if it were thought right for other reasons — without trial by jury. Whether one uses the Treason Act, or any other Act, one still has to have a trial with, in my view, a jury. If we were to abandon the Diplock courts in Northern Ireland, I believe that we could say goodbye to the majority of convictions for terrorism. We would have less, not greater, protection.

Moving from Northern Ireland to the general terrorist position in the United Kingdom as a whole, I do not believe that it can be argued with conviction that capital punishment would be a deterrent against a determined and vicious terrorist. Surely the experience of the past year or so has made that argument even clearer than it was before. We have seen nine or ten hunger strikers starve themselves to death in an Ulster gaol. One could not argue that they would have been deterred by the fear of death. They sought death for the purposes of their own perverted cause. How much more glamorous — if one may use the word in that horrible context — and effective for their perverted purposes it would have been had they met death upon a British gallows than the squalor of starving to death in a hospital bed. How much more frightening might have been the consequences for other people. How much more dangerous the repercussive elements might have been. I believe that in the vital category of terrorist crime the death penalty would not protect, but would further endanger innocent lives.

We have many other possible applications before us. Leaving aside the illogicality of proclaiming the unique value of the deterrent and then not being able to use it in cases of the worst form of slaughter, it has long been attractive to some people to seek different categories, despite the general disillusionment with the attempt to do that in the Homicide Act 1957, which lasted for seven years and proved extremely difficult to administer. What categories are raised? There are police and prison officers. Although numbers are small by international standards, it is a grave matter when a police officer is killed in the course of duty. There are too many such deaths.

But what are the most important aspects of the effectiveness of the police to combat crime? First, the understanding and support of the public. Secondly, the likelihood of the courts convicting the guilty whom the police have apprehended. I doubt whether capital punishment would help in either case. It would perhaps hinder. If there were a different and more severe punishment for killing policemen than for killing a civilian — perhaps a young girl bank clerk who endeavoured to resist a criminal and to uphold the law — would that help relations between the police and the public and the degree of mutual support which I regard as absolutely crucial?

Next, there is the likelihood of conviction. Police opinion on that matter is not unanimous. I am well aware of the position of the Police Federation, which I respect having had dealings with it over many years. I do not agree with its view on this matter — a view which it has held for a long time. There are others who take a different view.

In 1974 the Commissioner of Police of the Metropolis, without being asked by me, spontaneously stated that it was his view and that of four out of five of his most senior officers that capital punishment would be a hindrance, not a help. I have not inquired about the position since then. I do not believe that senior police officers should be canvassed in this respect. I tell the House that because the statement was volunteered to me. Why did they take that view? It was not, I think, out of softness, but for fear that capital punishment would make conviction more difficult to achieve and leave the police less well protected at the end of the day.

Another question, which is for the House, not the police, is that of majority verdicts in criminal trials. I introduced that provision into the Criminal Justice Act 1967 and it went through, but not without considerable opposition and difficulty in the House. It was something of a cross-party issue, although most of the opposition came from the Conservative benches. I make no great point about that. The present Prime Minster voted against.

It was a difficult change to introduce, but in my view it is now widely accepted. It has worked well and it is valuable and important in the fight against crime. More than ten per cent of convictions are now secured by majority verdicts. Those especially affected are the most hardened and professional criminals. Could we continue with majority verdicts in capital cases if the ultimate penalty was to result? It would be a difficult question to answer. And if we say that majority verdicts are not acceptable in one category of cases, might not that undermine the position in others?

There would be difficulty in obtaining convictions, not out of sentiment but occasionally because of corruption, supineness, or perhaps a scintilla of genuine doubt in the minds of the jury. Some possibilities of doubt are too great to be shrugged aside. I have been concerned with ten capital cases in which there were varying degrees of doubt. Some turned out to be wrongful convictions. Some cases raised doubt — sometimes substantial doubt — which led to it being clearly shown that there had been a miscarriage of justice. In others there was just a scintilla of doubt which left a lingering feeling of uncertainty. There have been one or two further cases since then. That is not a negligible proportion. During the twenty years after the Second World War when capital punishment existed, only 186 people were sentenced to death. Not all of the doubtful cases were hanged, but two were, and others might well have been.

That leads me to the conclusion that the death penalty is too final a punishment for the frailty of human judgement, especially as there is no convincing evidence that it would give greater security and a very strong argument that, in the major cases of terrorism, it would increase the danger.

In present circumstances, some may say 'Let us try anything, especially what the public wishes.' While I in no way dismiss popular views on this matter easily, that is not a responsible attitude for the House. We do not live in a plebiscitary democracy, except recently on rare major constitutional issues, nor should we. I hope that the House will exercise its courageous judgement tonight, as it has on previous occasions, and reject the new clauses.

Speech in the House of Commons, 1983

Mr Roy Jenkins (Glasgow, Hillhead). The speech of the Home Secretary — a speech comparable to two on this subject which I delivered from the same position during the 1970s — left me bewildered. He began by setting out the good, clear, reasonable test of saying: let us put old prejudices behind us and look at it afresh, and on the whole I would be prepared to go along with him on that — but he then proceeded, coolly and rationally — and to me persuasively — to destroy the case for capital punishment on all the amendments but one. Then he came to terrorism.

As soon as the right hon. and learned Gentleman did that, he galloped through — a sort of tribute to differing views in the Cabinet — a catalogue of the case put forward by the Secretary of State for Northern Ireland, but faced none of the issues involved in that case. He elided off into some general asseverations in which he completely deserted the test of public safety and the rational approach which he had previously applied. He went on to say that terrorist crimes had to be viewed with such repugnance, because they were crimes against the state, that we should not apply those rational tests but should use the final supreme penalty without regard to whether it would work or increase public safety.

There are enormous dangers in that approach. It implies that other crimes, however bestial they may be, are not regarded with the same repugnance. That is a dangerous view to take. It also means that we are moving away from looking at the matter clearly and coolly, as the right hon. and learned Gentleman started by doing. He made a good speech to begin with, but it was fatally flawed, and so it became a sorry performance at the end of the day.

The right hon. and learned Gentleman cannot get away with not answering the questions to clarify his position which were put to him by the right hon. Member for Birmingham, Sparkbrook (Mr Hattersley) and which I shall repeat, because if he does not answer them, I must tell him, as somebody who has twice occupied his office and spoken from the Dispatch Box in very similar circumstances, that he will be neglecting his duty to the House as Home Secretary.

I shall deal, because it is the essence of the matter, almost exclusively with the terrorism aspect, and I come immediately to the two points which the right hon. and learned Gentleman must answer. First, the vital issue is whether the supreme penalty — if that is what one is to call it — is to be used in Great Britain only or in Northern Ireland as well.

I remember that in a debate in 1974 the right hon. Gentleman who is now the Secretary of State for Education and Science put forward the extraordinary proposition that it should be used in Great Britain but not in Northern Ireland. I say 'extraordinary' because the nature of the threat in relation to the population is, on the record, six hundred times as great in Northern Ireland as it is in Great Britain.

It is, therefore, an extraordinary proposition to say that it is a uniquely valuable deterrent but that we should use it where the threat is relatively small and not use it where the threat is six hundred times greater. There could be no possibility, no basis in logic or morals, of doing that.

If, in the United Kingdom as a whole, including Northern Ireland, it were to apply, how would we obtain convictions? As we know, trials for terrorism in Northern Ireland are by the so-called Diplock courts, judges without juries, because is is almost impossible to get jury convictions for terrorism in the Province. Is the right hon. and learned Gentleman really saying that one could hang a man or woman —

Rev. Ian Paisley (Antrim, North) *rose*—

Mr Jenkins: Is the Home Secretary saying that, for the first time for centuries, one could hang a man or woman in a part of the United Kingdom without a jury trial?

Those are the two points on which we must have the clear view of the Home Secretary. Let me make the questions absolutely clear, so that there is no question of his dodging them. Is he proposing that the death penalty should be used in both Northern Ireland and Great Britain? Will he therefore abolish the Diplock courts and, if so, how would he hope to get convictions?

Mr Brittan: I am sorry that the right hon. Gentleman did not find it possible to get the answers that he seeks from my speech. Had he listened carefully he would have heard them. However, I am happy to deal with the matter in this way, though it is slightly curious that he should find it necessary to make allegations of an unfounded kind about whether or not one is prepared to answer his points.

I made it clear that I did not think it was possible to distinguish between Great Britain and Northern Ireland for these purposes. I also made it clear that I fully recognised the difficulties in relation to convictions by jury in Northern Ireland and that I did not expect that to be restored. I spoke of one possibility that had been mentioned — not by me, but by those who favoured this course — namely, that trials in Northern Ireland for offences of a capital kind should be conducted, not by a single judge but by a judge with assessors or by a panel of judges.

Mr Jenkins: It was not unreasonable of me to ask the right hon. and learned Gentleman to clarify that, because I do not think it was clear from his speech to any hon. Member (Hon. Members; 'Hear hear'). The right hon. and learned Gentleman is now saying, having clarified one point totally and satisfactorily, that there would be no distinction on either side of St George's Channel. The right hon. and learned Gentleman is also saying and this is less clear—

Mr Brittan *rose*—

Mr Jenkins: The right hon. and learned Gentleman should not be so impatient. He is floating a possible idea and not submitting a clear proposition. He has no idea whether the procedure of a judge and assessors would work, and he has no idea whether the judiciary would accept it. However, he is proposing that in the peculiarly delicate circumstances of Northern Ireland there should be hanging — as I have said, this would be for the first time for centuries — without trial by jury. That is one of the most extraordinary propositions that a Home Secretary or any other Cabinet Minister has ever put before the House.

Mr Nicholas Budgen (Wolverhampton, South-West): Will the right hon. Gentleman allow my right hon. and learned Friend the Home Secretary to say whether the judiciary in Northern Ireland has said that it would sit with assessors in accordance with the idea that he has floated?

Mr Jenkins: That is a relevant question, but it would probably be better if the hon. Gentleman were to put it to the Home Secretary in his own speech. I do not think that the system which the right hon. and learned Gentleman has proposed would work. If we are to have capital punishment for terrorist crimes, and if we are to extend that to Northern Ireland, we shall have to return to trial by jury in Northern Ireland. That will result almost certainly in terrorists being hanged occasionally, with the most dangerous repercussive effects. But the majority of terrorists would be acquitted and be free to carry on their nefarious trade.

I have no doubt that the dangerous repercussive effects of judicial killing for terrorist crimes in Northern Ireland, or in this country, could be devastating. That is why Lord Whitelaw, as he now is, abolished it in 1972. His reasons are set out in the statement that he put before the House in that year. Those reasons have convinced everyone, with the exception of one individual, who has had any responsibility in Northern Ireland over the past decade or so that many innocent lives might be endangered by employing judicial killing.

I had to deal with hunger strikes, including the hunger strike of the Price sisters, and I was enormously aware of the dangers, which should not be underestimated. The Price sisters were two girls who threatened to kill themselves. If the issue had been whether they were to be killed on the gallows, think how much more explosive the position would have been. Is there a balance between a dangerous repercussive effect and a deterrent effect? None of us is moving in a realm of absolute certainty, but that seems a particularly difficult case to argue in terms of terrorists, especially Irish terrorists.

A hunger strike that will lead to death is an immensely powerful and obvious example that is present in all our minds, and so I shall not weary the House with it. However, no one can pretend that being an Irish terrorist is a safe occupation. Irish terrorists kill themselves by the dozen, and always have done. In the Psychosis of Northern Ireland terrorism, death is the currency of the trade. No doubt the primary desire of terrorists is to deal it out to others, but they are also willing to accept it for themselves as part of their grisly trade. The place of the funeral in the mythology of Irish terrorism is an eloquent tribute to that.

There are some who will say that those considerations apply only to the hard core of fanatics. They acknowledge that by hanging we might create a few perversely triumphant martyrs, but argue that the essential supporting baggage train would be deterred. I do not agree with that argument. For example, we cannot hang landladies who provide safe houses. We cannot hang mothers who shelter their sons. We cannot hang women who shelter their husbands. We cannot hang boys of thirteen, fourteen or fifteen, and they would be increasingly involved in terrorism. No one is suggesting that we would do so and we must not pretend that we could. There is no question of the House or the country doing that. That being said, do not let us pretend that we can deter the baggage train. Do not let us pretend that we can do something that we cannot. Let us not deceive ourselves that we can create a great weapon of deterrence, only to face the humiliation of seeing it break in our hands.

Irish terrorists may be the primary problem, but the problem does not end there. One of the last acts of judicial execution in western Europe was carried out in Spain, where five terrorists were executed in October 1975. What was the deterrent effect? Nine policemen were shot in the following two weeks. I am convinced that hanging or any other form of judicial killing for terrorism would increase public danger rather than increase public safety. I do not go as far as that in respect of the other amendments, but the case in favour of them is unproven.

I, too, have had responsibility for the police. We all have a great regard for their exposed position. I am convinced that if the police were to be singled out for protection, public/police co-operation would be damaged. That co-operation is crucial to the success of the police in the front line in the fight against crime.

If we look back over the history of the capital punishment controversy,

I think the House will agree that the Bentley case, a police shooting case, was one of three cases to drive nails into the case for capital punishment and led to its abolition in the mid-1960s.

I hope that the House will vote clearly and consistently on all the propositions before it. There are some who might say that it would not matter if one or two votes went in contrary directions, for the subsequent legislation would never pass through Parliament. I certainly do not think that it would if the Home Secretary had responsibility for drafting it. That may be a tempting proposition for those who, like myself, do not wish the majority of the Government's legislative programme to pass through the House, but it would not be good in general. It would be bad for the Government's position, bad for Parliament, bad for the integrity of the law and bad for the protection of the public. Let us settle the issue in all its aspects, and let us do so now. We are a new Parliament and we have all been in recent contact with our constituencies. Presumably we have all made our views clear on these issues — certainly I have. Let us give a clear answer to the motion and all the amendments.

CHAPTER IV

Europe

Speech to the Royal Institute of International Affairs, Chatham House, 11 December 1980

The 1979 Dimbleby Lecture had been entitled 'Home Thoughts from Abroad'. It was made at a time when Roy Jenkins had served nearly three years of his Presidential term in Brussels and with just over a year to go before he returned to the British political scene. With less than a month of office remaining, on 11 December 1980, Jenkins delivered the last speech he was to make in Britain as President of the European Commission. It was at the Royal Institute of International Affairs in London that he tackled the central issue of why Britain should remain in the Community.

Let us be clear first that there should be no question — particularly on the part of those who want us to come out — of denying the importance of the issue. Eight years ago these same people were in the forefront of the demand for a referendum on Britain's membership. And they justified this constitutional innovation precisely on the grounds of the exceptional importance and permanence of the decision: that it would set Britain's policy course for a generation and more. Five and a half years ago they had their referendum, with its high turn-out and massive majority for continued membership. The argument of permanence, it now appears, was merely a device for getting a referendum — which it was thought would give a very different result. So far from its result being accepted, it is now proposed, a mere quinquennium later and proposed by Britain's only apparent alternative government, as a result of a motion carried after only forty minutes of cursory debate, that the country should completely change its external policy tack at the earliest opportunity. And it is also proposed that this should be done without even a further referendum to legitimise, if that were the outcome, the undoing of the result of the former one. The referendum, having failed to serve its purpose for the 'antis' in 1975, would be discarded into the constitutional waste paper basket. This is both a frivolous and an undemocratic approach to policy making. I did not like the referendum in the first place, but to reverse its result without re-applying its method would be constitutional trickery.

There is another consideration. Apart from the merits of the issue, which I will come to in a moment, it is essential if this country is to have any faithful friends to whom it can turn in time of trouble, and if it is to exercise, in its post-imperial and somewhat impoverished state, any continuing influence in the world, that it should have a reputation for constancy of purpose and reliability of resolve. Such qualities were indeed, partly as a result of our wartime efforts, thought to be some of the most valuable which we carried into the post-war world. They are also qualities which are at a premium in the dangerous world of today. Are they dependable, are their policies predictable? These are questions I have constantly heard asked with searching concern, and not only about us, by the most significant of world leaders. Yet what shred of reputation for constancy would we have if, after trying to get into the Community for twelve years, after then renegotiating the terms of entry, then putting the result to a referendum to settle it permanently, then demanding — with justice — and getting a much better budget settlement, we were to turn round like squirrels in a cage and say we are off again? You simply cannot be a serious factor in world affairs upon such a fluctuating basis.

I do not believe there is a very great danger of that occurring. For reasons I have already given I think it would be a constitutional monstrosity to come out without a further referendum — although it would be highly undesirable, from the point of view of our influence in the meantime, to create the uncertainty of even another referendum. We have after all decided that once. But if there had to be a referendum I believe that when the issues were expounded and faced the British people would decide as they did last time, although perhaps by a less decisive majority and after a somewhat more uphill argument. Why is that? Why, in other words, are many sections of British opinion at least superficially more disenchanted with the Community than is any comparable body of opinion in any of the other eight countries? As it is always desirable to understand the other side's case and not to rely upon abusing his attorney, I set out what I believe to be the main reasons for this.

First, we are a somewhat insular people with a strong sense of national identity — but not more than the French, who manage to achieve insularity without being an island, but also manage to be strongly nationalistic without raising any question of their not being an integral part of the Community. This is not therefore a decisive factor.

What is much more to the point is the second consideration. By a combination of miscalculation and ill-fortune we entered the Community at almost the worst possible moment. British Governments were responsible for our not being in at the creation, when we would have been wholly welcome and could have played a major part in the formulation of the shape and rules of the Community. Then in the sixties, when we belatedly saw our mistake, De Gaulle would not have us in. By 1973 we were at the end of the relatively easy years and the long surge to prosperity which for all the original Six had marked their first fifteen years of membership of the Community, transformed their standards of living, and made nearly all of them, for the first time since the industrial revolution, substantially richer than were we. This experience has given them all a fundamental loyalty to the Community. We did not fully share in the surge to prosperity, and we did not share in it at all from within the Community. And from 1973 onwards, partly as a result of the first oil crisis, now more than reinforced by the second, the world has been a much harsher place, with increased prosperity much more difficult to achieve. Our first years in the Community were not good years for anyone, and our own performance was worse than most.

This consideration of timing also applied to the other two, Ireland and Denmark, who entered with us. But they are distinguished from us by the fact that the Community system of financing, both on the expenditure and the resources sides, as it had evolved prior to our entry, was of natural benefit to their economies. It was not so for us. We were not unique amongst the Nine in that respect. Germany was not a natural direct beneficiary, but her economy had made the fullest use of the indirect benefits of a single market. We were unique in two respects. One was in the unlucky timing of our delayed entry. The other was the setting of a budgetary mould, partly because we were not there at the beginning, which could only be tinkered with and not fundamentally changed during both the entry negotiations of 1970-2 and the renegotiations of 1974-5, and which did not suit us.

And there are further considerations. There is the fact that Mrs Thatcher's budgetary negotiation of the past year, successful though it was, was conducted in such a way as to encourage an 'us against them' mentality. There is also the fact that the Community like all human institutions has its imperfections, and perhaps because of its inevitable complications, a little more than most. Seen from Britain it all seems remote and alien. All these circumstances, in my view, go far to explain the greater difficulties of reconciling British opinion to the Community than is the case in any other member or candidate country.

So much for analysis. Why does it not follow from it that it would be best to recognise the differences as irreconcilable, and, as amicably as possible, to call it a day? Essentially, for three reasons, each of which would in my view be sufficient in itself, but which are together overwhelming.

First, the Community may be called the European *Economic* Community but it has always been a Community which sought political ends through economic means. Its central purpose has been to put behind us the old quarrels which nearly destroyed Western Europe over several generations and threw away its old prosperity and its old influence in the world. The enmities have been triumphantly buried. But the need for a common European voice and a common European foreign policy is still greater today than it was when we entered the Community, greater than it was when we voted to stay in 1975. Every event that occurs in the world underlines that need. It is a much more dangerous world — from Afghanistan to Poland to the Iran-Iraq conflict. It is a world of much less certain American leadership, inevitable to some extent since the end of the long period of almost effortless captaincy of the West a decade ago, but accentuated by having four Presidents in six-and-a-half years — a rate of change unprecedented in this century. It is a world in which the North/South relationship becomes at once increasingly vital and difficult, and in which the Community is a major and constructive factor. The need therefore for foreign policy co-ordination, for a common approach of the Nine, is greater than it ever was before. But it is not only a need. It is also a reality. Political co-operation, as it is called in the jargon of the Community, has bounded forward in the past year as it never has before. It is now central to the meetings of Heads of Government and of Foreign Ministers. Britain plays a leading role. For us to exclude ourselves from this at the present time would not merely be unwise. It would be almost insane. We would become lonely and isolated, sharing in all the risks of Continental Europe but not participating in its power, half wanting to make for the eastern shores of America, but uncertain of our strength to get there, and doubtful of our welcome if we arrived.

Economically the case for British membership of the Community has always been a little more balanced than the political case. That was recognised in the successive White Papers which were published by different British Governments between the early sixties and the middle seventies. It was certainly recognised in the speeches which, as President of Britain In Europe. I made in the 1975 referendum campaign, as in those of many others. Yet paradoxically perhaps, the economic case is stronger today than it ever has been. After seven rather lean trading years with Europe, assuaged by some regional and social policy advantages which could have been greater had successive British Governments tried harder, we are now getting substantial trading benefits. Forty-three per cent of our exports go to the rest of the Community. Germany is our first export market — bigger now than the United States, although with little more than a quarter of the population. Six of our other nine best export markets are within the other seven members of the Community. Our visible trade balance with the Community has improved strikingly. We now cover ninety-four per cent of our imports from the rest of the Community with exports, compared with only seventy per cent in 1975, and our invisibles do very well too. To take ourselves out of the integrated Community market now would be to throw away just at the moment of take-off much of the accumulated effort of our firms' imports and exports over the past eight years.

It is not merely a question of trading relationships within Europe. The Community is made increasingly responsible for problem industries: steel at the insistent request of the British Government, amongst others; textiles, where we will soon have to re-negotiate with difficulty the Multi-Fibre Agreement; shipbuilding, the problems of which are manifest. Britain has more than her fair share of these old industries in difficulty, and she certainly cannot solve their problems on her own. But it is unsatisfactory and unlikely that the Community can just be left to look after lame ducks. If Europe, or any of its Member States, is to be in the front rank of industrial powers in the 1990s it must make a determined and united effort to catch up the ground it has lost both to the United States and to Japan in the new micro-electronic or 'telematique' wave of industrial innovation. That can only be done within a continental framework. No individual European country market is big enough. The Community cannot do it all. A lot must be left to the enterprise of companies. But the framework of common standards and the massive backing of public purchasing must be European. Unless this is done we shall certainly not maintain the standard of living to which we are used in Europe. We shall be squeezed from above and below. And those outside the common enterprise will be worse squeezed than those within.

There is a third consideration. The Community is now more poised for change than at any time since its first beginnings — when we in Britain so wantonly threw away our capacity to help make its shape. In the negotiations for our entry in the early seventies a lot of problems were put off to the future. That future has now arrived, and is recognised to have done so by nearly every government in the Community, but perhaps most notably by the Government of the Federal Republic of Germany. The CAP, the Community budget as a whole, are open to radical reform. The imbalance, which was the British budget problem now transferred in part to Germany; the exhaustion of the existing forms of 'own resources'; the imminence of a major enlargement of the Community to the South all make that inevitable.

In the next eighteen months Britain has more to play for in the Community, with a better chance of allies, than at any time since her entry. Now at last we could play a role in the shaping of the Community such as has not been possible since we failed to go to the Messina Conference of 1955 which led on to the Treaty of Rome in 1957 in which we took no part. It is rare that the opportunity to be 'a born-again' innovator comes to a nation a second time. But we cannot achieve it without a whole-hearted commitment, without giving a sense of being a dependable and not a fluctuating partner. As our political and, now, our trading interests point so firmly in the same direction, it would be ludicrous to miss the opportunity. As I argued earlier, through a fault partly but by no means entirely our own, we went into the Community at an unfortunate time. To think about coming out now would be to compound that national miscalculation on a scale which has been rarely seen in history.

Britain and Europe - A Ten-year Appraisal

The themes of the Chatham House lecture were repeated many times during the following years. The Declaration for Social Democracy of January 1981 included a phrase that Social Democrats wanted Britain to play a full and constructive role within the framework of the European Community. Attitudes to Europe were part of the cement that bound together the membership of the new SDP. Most Social Democrats were dismayed at the xenophobic attitudes of so much of the country. This was accentuated by Tory opportunism, and Labour's downright hostility — based upon whatever arguments came to hand – against closer ties with Europe. The former Labour MPs who joined the SDP included the most 'communitaire' amongst the Parliamentary Labour Party and numbered many of those who had voted with Roy Jenkins for entry in defiance of the Labour Whip, in October 1971.

The attitude to Europe was again a great binding force within the Alliance. Until 1981 the Liberals had been alone in approaching the relationship with Europe in a constructive, far-sighted and idealistic way. The Alliance seized this common ground as one of its main identifying characteristics. It also highlighted an area of major difference with the Labour Party as the alternative to Conservative governments.

Many of Roy Jenkins' major speeches, through his two by-election campaigns, in support of Alliance by-election candidates and through the 1983 General Election, consistently brought out the importance of the European relationship to the future of the United Kingdom.

In June 1984 the second European Parliamentary elections took place and four months before that, on 27 February, Jenkins delivered a major speech at a Financial Times *Conference.*

As I shall make some fairly critical remarks about the present state of the European Community and the present leadership of the European Community, perhaps I should begin by setting out two points. First, I do not for one moment believe that it will disintegrate. What there is a real danger of is that it will stagnate, and maybe even recede a little. But that is quite different from actually breaking up, because the intertwined entrenched interests, in my view, are now far too strong for there to be any question of it actually breaking up. Secondly, perhaps I ought to say that in my view the case for Britain coming out remains preposterous, both from a trade and an inward investment point of view, and from the fact that deliberately to introduce a major element of instability at the present dangerous time in the world, into one of the relatively few areas of the world which is reasonably stable, would be an act of frivolitiy almost beyond belief.

Having said that I turn to a slightly more critical view of the present position. In the past two or three weeks I have been reading a lot and writing a little about the creation of NATO which took place thirty-five years ago, and which you may have seen if you read an intermittent series of articles in *The Times* this spring. It is a remarkable story. It was all put together in fifteen months. Twelve founder members signed the treaty fifteen months after the first serious negotiations had begun. As this fifteen months was bisected almost exactly by a presidential election in the United States, in which the incumbent was thought almost certain to lose before he actually won, and as the United States was the country which had to make incomparably the biggest contribution in terms both of resources and of sacrifice of tradition, it really was a prodigious feat of political engineering to put it together.

The reason I mention that is to contrast the present performance of the governments, heads of governments and members of governments of the ten Community countries who have succeeded now, with a lot of help from this country, in turning every successive meeting into an accountant's wrangle. This looks not merely petty-minded but a disgraceful abdication of leadership. If they and not their wider-perspective forebears had been in charge of North Atlantic affairs thirty-five years ago I doubt if America would ever have been committed to Europe, if Berlin would have been saved, the Marshall Plan implemented, European recovery got under way, and European security underpinned.

This does not mean that the Community must run away from its financial problems. It cannot do so now; it cannot avoid them. It has to face up to them. But the idea that everything previously was a sort of careless rapturous path of champagne and roses is absolute nonsense. The idea that a price freeze for agriculture is something quite new is not true. The Commission — my Commission, if I may say so — put forward an agricultural price freeze for 1979, and very small increases well below

K

the rate of inflation for the other three years. It was the governments which sold out for higher levels of price increase.

In dealing with these budgetary problems it is important to realise, as I am sure you all do, that the problem of agricultural expenditure being out of control is not the same as the British budgetary problem, although it impacts upon it. They are two separate problems which overlap for a relatively small part of their circumference. So far as the agricultural expenditure is concerned it is undesirable that agricultural expenditure should take over sixty per cent of the budget of a Community that earns over ninety per cent of its living from industry and commerce, and unacceptable that it can surge up out of control towards seventy per cent. In my view agricultural expenditure must now be firmly sealed off, though as with many things in life one wishes that one had not got to this point, but having got there it is an illusion to believe that one can in practice greatly reduce it as opposed to sealing off any further increases.

But it should be said that it does not follow from this that the Common Agricultural Policy has little or nothing to be said for it. Nor does it follow that European agriculture is exceptionally either subsidised or protected. It is done in somewhat perverse ways, but compared with either the United States or Japanese agriculture it is certainly not out of line, and maybe not as subsidised or protected as the agriculture of either of the two other major industrial blocs in the world.

The Community Agricultural Policy also has considerable achievements to its credit. It has brought about great improvements in efficiency. It has led to many millions of people going off the land, which was thought a good thing at any rate in the days of full employment, though about whether one wants any more people off the land I am increasingly sceptical. It has also produced a roughly equivalent standard of living in town and country for the first time in Western Europe, including this country, since the New World supplies came in over a century ago. There are excesses at the edges but these are quite considerable achievements. Nor should we deceive ourselves that any return to the old British system of farm support would save money, or that you can take apart the unity of the agricultural market without beginning to unravel the unity — not complete, but substantial — of the industrial market as well.

What is wrong with the agricultural budget and has produced the imbalance is the historical misfortune that most help to agriculture is done through the Community budget as such, and only a very small proportion of other forms of expenditure, whether it be regional policy or industrial innovation or even propping up the old industries — I am more interested in assisting new industries at the present time — is done through national budgets and not through the Community. I believe that in these circumstances the British Government is right in saying that you must seal off agricultural expenditure. The haemorrhage must be stopped. I would not be yielding on this. But it is also necessary, if the Community budget is to have any sensible shape, that you also substantially extend those other forms of activity which I have mentioned. Apart from anything else, from a purely British point of view it is the only way in which you can get the British problem corrected, as it were organically, naturally, at source. That is the only way which will really work from the point of view of providing a permanent solution with Britain's influence enhanced rather than reduced by it in the Community. To go on negotiating and renegotiating a special subvention each year is something which has become totally unsatisfactory and is deeply debilitating for Britain's influence within the Community. It is fair; it is reasonable; but it is always the extras on the bill which irritate people. The special subvention is an extra on the bill for our Community partners and we pay, in my view, a heavy price for it. You cannot do it on the basis of *juste retour*, which would involve a whole series of restrictive arrangements, to make sure that everyone gets out exactly what they put in. That would be like trying to run an irrigation scheme, while making sure that water never got to any land beyond the little canal in which it was contained to begin with. It would be totally destructive of any recovery of momentum within the Community.

But I go beyond that and would say that, having been unrelenting on getting control of agricultural expenditure, I would be relatively relaxed on the exact British budgetary payment. Of course nobody thinks it reasonable, nobody on either side of the Channel, that you should go back to the vast imbalance which was developing in 1980, when we were paying £1,000 million to £1,200 million more than we were getting out. But what is at issue are much more limited sums — a couple of hundred million pounds one way or the other. Britain has a great and not ignoble — rather the reverse — desire to play a part in world affairs and to exercise an influence. We spend very substantial amounts of money in, looked at from some points of view, purchasing influence in the world. We spend £14 billion a year on defence, and I hope that that is more for influence than for destruction. We are about to spend £12 billion spread over a period on a new weapon system, about which I am very sceptical. We have suggested spending £1 billion a year on a dual safety catch for cruise missiles, using 'we' there in the sense of the Alliance, the Social Democrat Party. We spend getting on for £1 billion a year on the Falklands. These are all expenditures of substantial sums of money on foreign policy influence. In my view an investment of a few hundred million, which is relatively small in relation to these expenditures, might at the present time pay very substantial dividends. Europe has never been so bereft of leadership since the war as it is today, and is a particularly unfortunate time for this to be so. If one looks back over the postwar period there was at first that very remarkable trio of three leaders from the core of Europe who put the Community together. There was Alcide de Gaspari from Italy. Konrad Adenauer from Germany, Robert Schuman from France. They all came from the parts of their countries which were nearest to other countries and, a remarkable fact, no less than tow of them, de Gaspari and Schuman, had lived their early lives in empires different from the countries they later governed. De Gaspari actually sat in the Austro-Hungarian Diet and Schuman was a German citizen until 1918. They provided a federalist — catholic, if you like — core of leadership in the early days, buttressed by Spaak of Belgium and by the quiet innovative genius of Jean Monnet who was a Frenchman from the shores of the Atlantic and not from the centre of Europe.

Later you had a phase in which the leadership was less unified, where you had Hallstein as the most powerful President of the Commission and de Gaulle, not working all that closely together — the pope and the emperor, as they were sometimes known; it is not necessary to define which was which — contesting for supremacy in Europe, But at that stage the momentum — the momentum of the great surge to growth in Europe in the sixties — was such that it could carry conflicts within the leadership.

Then in the mid seventies through into the early, very early eighties, you had the partnership of Helmut Schmidt and Giscard d'Estaing, which provided an axis of leadership. Sometimes it was too close. It could sometimes be too negative; it was uncomfortable for some other people, it was uncomfortable for the British, it was uncomfortable for the smaller countries, because it is difficult to cluster around an axis. It is easier to do it round and within a triangle. It is a great pity that the British did not form a triangle. At any rate, the axis provided discernible leadership. When they wanted to move something forward, they could, as with the European Monetary System. When they wanted to block something, it was blocked.

But now there is nothing. There is a vacuum. There is a vacuum such as there has not been for thirty-five or forty years past. I believe that it is essential that we should try to move in and get something moving forward. It is a great error of the British that we have — first by staying out and then by being kept out, then hovering as we have more recently on the threshold, not like a full partner but more like an uncertain guest — thrown away our opportunities to provide that triangle of leadership which I think might get a great response from a variety of countries.

I believe at the present time the Community needs to become more political — not in a party sense, obviously, but in the proper meaning of the word — more concerned with defence, more concerned with arms control. Again, if one looks back for a moment at the history of NATO one sees that during the early years of that remarkable but on the whole very successful alliance, starting from a position of almost total American preponderance in every field — military, economic, monetary — in every field there was total American preponderance in the early years of the alliance — but then from about the mid-fifties onwards through to the mid- or even late seventies there then proceeded to be a very substantial eastward or Cisatlantic shift in the balance of power within the alliance. This applied in every sphere except that of nuclear strike power, which itself became less important, though not less dangerous, as the Soviet Union moved towards a position of equality. But in every other field Europe became both relatively and absolutely stronger and the United States relatively weaker. The factors here were the emergence of the Federal Republic — it was not there at all at the beginning of the alliance — not only as an economic wonder but also as a substantial conventional land power as well. The unprecedented general European surge to prosperity associated with the first fifteen years of the Community, then the weak dollar and somewhat apologetic tone, although the often far from foolish actions of the Carter presidency, all contributed to this process. It was fortified by the strong growth of political co-operation in Europe. It was epitomised by Helmut Schmidt lecturing President Carter more in sorrow than anger, in a way that it would have been impossible to imagine Adenauer doing with Eisenhower. It was statistically supported by the Community overtaking the United States in total income.

That phase now looks to be over. Already, to take the last point first, the combined national income of the Community countries has fallen back to ninety-three per cent of that of the United States. Short-term that gap is at the moment widening daily, but the longer-term prospect seems to be much more serious, with Europe falling behind in the technology of the new industrial revolution to such an extent as to make it highly uncertain whether we can keep in the same league as either Japan or the United States. The much talked of strengthening of the European pillar of the alliance is not merely not happening; such strength as the pillar had is being eroded rather than increased.

I think in these circumstances to spend all our time in Europe quibbling about a few hundreds of millions of pounds is something which in the context of wider issues looks totally disproportionate. There are major developments, some of them good, some of them bad, going on in the world at the present time. We see a United States in which those from the western part of the continent are becoming much more powerful in the government, in positions of power in business and elsewhere, than has been the case throughout most of our lifetimes. We see a position in which the Pacific basin is being widely regarded as the great growth area of the world. We see a position in which Henry Kissinger is today reported as having advocated the withdrawal of half the United States' troops from Europe. In these circumstances the challenge to us in Europe, politically and from a defence point of view, is to get our head out of the groceries and to look to our political future. So far from providing a stronger pillar for the western alliance — which I firmly believe must continue to be an Atlantic alliance — we have recently lost our way in the relatively small issues with which the Community has concerned itself far too much.

Can the New European Parliament do better?

In Britain, although not in Northern Ireland, the June 1984 European elections took place on the first-past-the-post system. As intended by an unholy alliance of Conservative and Labour parties, this and a characteristically low poll effectively squeezed out any possibility of Alliance candidates, Social Democrat or Liberal, being elected. On the Continent of Europe, of course, many parties with a smaller percentage of votes cast achieved electoral success. The election of only the second European Parliament was an opportunity both to assess the record of its predecessor and to question the role of the European Parliament within the tripod of the Community's governing institutions. As the former President of the Commission, therefore, with great personal experience of dealing with the Parliament, Roy Jenkins was in a rare position to make such assessments. He did so in an article in the September 1984 edition of New Democratic *magazine.*

The first democratically elected European Parliament was a disappointment. Can the new Parliament avoid the same fate?

The first Parliament assembled in Strasbourg on 17 July 1979, in an atmosphere of eager anticipation, even an approach to excitement. Britain, alas, apart, there had been a good turnout in the elections and from nearly every other country the most notable figures who were not disqualified by government office had been elected.

France headed the list with no less than five former and future Prime Ministers — Edgar Faure, Pflimlin, Debré, Chirac and Mauroy — as well as Simone Veil, Delors and Marchais. Italy had Colombo, Craxi, Berlinguer and Spinelli. Germany had Brandt but no Christian

Democrat names of equal note, unless Bismarck and Hapsburg were thought to carry a resonance beyond their individual quality. Belgium had Tindemans, the Netherlands Vonderling.

Britain, with its already demoralised Labour Party and distorting electoral system, produced a Tory group of inflated size and considerable quality, but containing no politician whose name was known south and east of Dover — and few whose name was known north or west of it. Mrs Castle was alone in having to sustain the reputation of the poor but honest class of professional politician and did it remarkably well, with a fierce flair, from an isolated position.

As President of the Commission I approached the new Parliament, which I had to address twice in its first two days, with a mixture of hope and apprehension; hope, because I thought that it could sustain and increase the moderate momentum which Europe, with some recent industrial recovery, the European Monetary System (EMS) in place, and an increasing emphasis on political co-operation, had regained in the previous eighteen months; and apprehension because I knew that the Parliament's only two real powers were to reject the budget and to sack the Commission. Obviously it was going to sting in at least one direction, and the more logical one was to attack the Council of Ministers by rejecting the budget. However, as frustration was inevitable for such a grandly constituted assembly with such limited powers, it might easily have done so in both.

In the event it did not. It rejected almost unanimously its first budget in December 1979, and in so doing achieved its finest hour. Statements almost worthy of Pym and Hampden were made from diverse nationalities and diverse political groups. The trouble, was, however, that the Parliament had the negative courage and cohesion to reject a budget, but lacked the positive courage or cohesion to produce a viable alternative. Agriculture, as usual, was the lion in the path.

Thereafter that Parliament began to lose its zest. Its term roughly coincided with a quinquennium of bad-tempered and petty-minded stagnation in Europe. The Parliament did not cause this, but it lacked the leverage to avert it. It had a distinguished first President in Madame Veil, but most of its other members of note drifted into resignation or non-attendance. Short of powers, and not knowing quite how to use the limited ones which it had, it failed — a very few occasions excepted — to be a powerful sounding-board for great issues. This is a fate which it has shared with many other legislatures in the world. But it was the more serious for the European Parliament because it did not even have the consolation of being a legislature. It is no accident that of the sixteen 'notables' mentioned earlier, only three will be present in Strasbourg this week.

How can this new Parliament redress the failures of the old? The question, as is unfortunately so often the case, has to be answered from a different angle for a British than for a general European audience. The common British reaction is that if ever the Parliament is caught trying to do anything about anything — be it Northern Ireland, co-ordination of weapons production, harmonisation of standards in goods and services, the development of regional and social policies, a mild suggestion (probably, alas, now too late because too expensive) that it might be safer if we all drove on the same side of the road — it should be told to stop. As British interests in the community are for greater political content, for a more perfect market for goods and particularly services, and for a changed pattern of expenditure which breaks away from the old agricultural hegemony, such minimalism seems perverse.

In most of the other member states, by contrast, the Parliament would be widely accused of doing too little. This, it must be said, was not universally so. Helmut Schmidt and Valéry Giscard d'Estaing, good Europeans in general, believed they knew how to do it all without interference from a presumptuous Parliament.

Europe has become bogged down in detail and now lacks leadership, although Mitterrand is beginning to emerge as an exception. Meanwhile the Parliament is unesteemed. The best recipe for improving its reputation would be to moderate the excessive and rather meaningless rigidity of its party group system, and to try to find a single home and a common system of election. Most important of all, it should try to drag member governments back to facing the big issues, such as Europe's recent relative decline in relation to both Japan and the United States, and not to allow them to get lost in a delta of detail.

Europe in the Year 2000

In January 1985 New Democrat *magazine featured a series of articles on the theme 'Towards the 21st Century'. It seemed appropriate that Roy Jenkins, with his long personal history of involvement with the European Community over the thirty years since its inception, should be asked to contribute a view of Europe in the year 2000.*

What kind of Europe will we have in the year 2000? A glorified customs union or a major world economic force comparable to the United States of America in the twentieth century? How many members will there be —more or fewer than at present? And which will they be?

Only fifteen years remain of the twentieth century — a century in which until 1945 the European nations would have been at the top of any league for mutual slaughter and for involving the rest of the world in their internecine wars.

It is now more than thirty years since the first tentative steps towards the establishment of a European Community were taken. And in spite of apparently endless recent bickerings within the Community and some serious squabbles with our allies, it is a certainty, whatever other perils may await us, that we shall see out this century without one Community country taking up arms against another. The second half of the century, in sharp contrast with the first, will have witnessed a Western Europe which is one of the most stable and peaceful areas in the world. Given our history, that is a considerable achievement. What some regard as less certain, though I would be prepared to put more than a few ECUs on such a prediction, is that the European Community in roughly its present form will survive well beyond the year 2000. It is stagnation I fear, not disintegration.

What are the most important challenges which must be faced before the close of the twentieth century? There are I believe three which are so vital that, if we fail to grapple with them even by the end of this decade, they may well threaten Europe's future.

The first of these challenges is that of the enlargement of the Community. In its first fifteen years the original six member states achieved what was probably the biggest surge in prosperity ever seen in recorded history. The only possible rival achievement is the massive industrialisation in the United States after the Civil War. The original Six know very well how much they owe to that initial fifteen years of the Community. Britain was not a member at the time, largely through its own fault, and did not participate in the surge. It joined, together with Denmark and Ireland, only in 1973. That difference of experience goes a long way to account for the different and less favourable perception of the Community in Britain compared with that in the Six.

The Community is now one of ten member states, Greece having joined in 1981. Spain and Portugal are now due, after several postponements, to join in 1986. There are those who argue that if the ten member states already have such difficulty in reaching agreement on even minor issues, what hope can a Community of twelve ever have of making any progress. Spain and Portugal, they suggest, should therefore be denied entry. There is a certain superficial attraction in that argument. But I believe that it is dangerously wrong. First because Spain and Portugal are fully qualified for membership. They are European. They are now democratic. And they want to join. Any further postponement of their admission could jeopardise the stability of the recent and therefore inevitably fragile democratic regimes. This would be very much against the general European — and indeed Atlantic — interest.

There is sad irony in seeing Greece, the most recent member of the EEC, which attached great importance to an early date for its own entry, trying to delay further the admission of two other Mediterranean and relatively poor states. This may however drive home in the other countries, including particularly Britain, a valuable lesson. It has drawn attention to the impossibility of continuing even in a Community of Ten, with a system of unanimous decision making. Under the Treaty of Rome nearly all decisions were to be taken by a 'weighted majority'. That in practice has degenerated since the so-called Luxemburg Compromise of 1966 into the habit of the constant use of a one-country veto. I believe that major peril awaits the EEC if a decision is not soon taken to revert to the original system. Without such a change a Community of Twelve could indeed be a recipe for a stagnant Community.

The second area in which lie both peril and opportunity is that of the monetary role of the Community. Europe, after the collapse of the Bretton Woods system in 1971, suffered much more gravely from the currency fluctuations than did either the United States or Japan. For our two main competitors the fluctuations were external. For Europe they were internal. It is as though in the United States they had had a New York dollar, a San Francisco dollar, a Chicago dollar, an Atlanta dollar, each moving violently and often irrationally against the others. Under such conditions the United States would I believe have enjoyed a much less robust economic performance in the recent past.

In 1979 the Community put together the European Monetary System. It did it quickly — little more than a year from conception to birth. It was, but I trust will not remain, the last major Community initiative. The EMS did not aim at producing completely fixed exchange rates between the eight fully participating currencies. It did however produce a greater degree of exchange rate stability than there had hitherto been. Britain, regrettably, did not fully join the EMS. I believe that Britain suffered as a result. In 1980 and 1981 we had a pound sterling which was far higher than was healthy for our industry. With the rundown of our oil surplus we now face an extremely uncertain exchange rate. It would be to the advantage of the United Kingdom and Europe as a whole for Britain to become a full member. Although to a considerable extent the mark has taken over from sterling the leading European currency position, London remains the dominant financial centre in Europe, and any European monetary bloc is incomplete without it.

The third area of peril for Europe is that of its performance in the new technologies. There is an element of irony in the fact that while the members of the EEC have spent so much time and energy in grappling with the minutiae of creating a single market, our competitors have overtaken us in exploiting its advantages. Thus of every ten personal computers sold in Europe, eight were manufactured in the United States. Of every ten video-recorders, nine were made in Japan. European manufacturers of integrated circuits control only thirty per cent of world sales. In the industry as a whole the Community supplies only ten per cent of the world market, but takes in about one third of world sales. As recently as 1975 the Community's balance of payments in the area of information technology was positive. By 1982 it was in deficit to the tune of $10 billion. This is an area which requires vast resources of brain power in which the Community is rich, and little energy or raw materials in which it is relatively poor. Europe's failure even to satisfy its own domestic needs has important employment as well as balance of payment implications.

Europe has recently been too obsessed with accountancy. Value for money is important. But the total of the Community budget is only two per cent of public expenditure in the member states. Rather more than that is lost each year through frontier delays. Far more than that is lost through our failure to exploit the advantages of a unified market of nearly 300 million people for the new high technology industries.

If we are to be confident of our future up until and beyond the year 2000 we must get our head out of the groceries and regain the vision, nerve and perspective of those who more than thirty years ago were responsible for the European Community's creation.

CHAPTER V

Constitutional Reform

Fair Votes

On 14 September 1983 Roy Jenkins addressed the SDP Council for Social Democracy at the University of Salford.

The case against the present electoral system is powerful and obvious. It produces a House of Commons which is unrepresentative of opinion in the country. At the last election it took 33,000 votes to elect a Conservative MP, 40,000 to elect a Labour MP and 340,000 to elect an Alliance MP. That would be difficult to justify in logic or morals.

But the unfairness is not just against the Alliance. Last June the wild blade of the first-past-the-post system cut overwhelmingly against us. But if we move up against the Labour Party in this Parliament even half as fast as we did in the last Parliament, it is they who could be the next sufferers. And if the Conservative Party had to fight in the circumstances of Warrington or Crosby it is they who could be nearly annihilated. The consistent unfairness is not against one party or another. It is against the voters. It is they who do not get what they want, and what they vote for.

Nor is it simply a question of unfairness. It is also inefficient because it can, and has, produced damaging major reversals of policy based upon relatively minor shifts of opinion.

It is in addition dangerous because it could produce an extremist Government with an absolute majority in the House of Commons, but based not merely on a minority, but on a very small minority of the electorate. The Labour Government of 1974 was based on only twenty-eight per cent of the total electorate. Twenty-three per cent or twenty-four per cent could in certain circumstances be enough to do it in the future.

Furthermore the system is damaging to the social and geographical cohesion of the nation. It is not right that the Conservatives should not have a single seat in Glasgow or Liverpool. It is not right that Labour MPs should be almost completely non-existent in the South of England. But this is not merely wrong in some abstract sense. It makes one of the great parties a stranger to the suburbs, the countryside and the areas of relative prosperity. It makes another alien to the industrial wastelands and the regions of deprivation. It helps to tear the country apart.

We are a unifying bridge, and proud to be one. But that is not enough, for we suffer in terms of seats for the fairly even spread of our appeal, which is in itself a virtue. It is the system itself which is rotten.

But it has worked well in the past, some will claim. Why are you only complaining about it now? There are clear answers. First, the present system worked well only so long as there were two parties which between them had an almost total command over the votes and even the enthusiasm of the overwhelmingly majority of the electorate. That was so in the early fifties but has gradually ceased to be so. And now, with a full three grouping appeal, the system has become a mixture between a farce and a lottery. Before that period of two-party dominance there was a ferment of ideas for reform. One measure got through the House of Commons under the Labour Government of 1929-31, but failed in the House of Lords. Others were widely supported in the Conservative Party, and of course by the Liberal Party as well. Nor is it the case that we now in the SDP are all 'johnnies come lately' to this cause. In 1974, within six weeks of again becoming Home Secretary, I put forward a paper in favour of electoral reform to the Cabinet. It did not get much of a reception. Barbara Castle is my witness, intentionally hostile but in fact very helpful. She records the incident in her *Diaries:* 'We sent Roy away with a flea in his coalition ear', she dismissively concludes.

What are the other arguments against the change? It is always a good idea to try to understand the other side's case. Basically the arguments against are that the present system produces strong, effective, coherent government, and that it preserves the relationship of the individual MP with a single constituency.

But do we really believe that we have been more effectively and coherently governed over the past two decades than the West Germans with their very sensible system of proportional representation? Nor has that system produced small splinter parties. They have fewer such parties with PR than we have without.

In any event let us not forget that one of the first elections to be fought will be the European election. In that case there is no question of a Government being created or elected. And yet many people led by Mrs Thatcher remain adamantly against a fairer system even in those European elections. There is no possible argument for Mrs Thatcher on this except the claim that it is the thin end of the wedge: a delicate argument to use at this conference, but one which must be rejected. The case for the European elections is an overwhelming one.

There is the single-MP, single-constituency argument. It must first be said that there is no known system of representation on land or sea which is perfect. All have some faults. But some have a great many more than others.

The advantages of single-member constituencies can be exaggerated.

Where they are natural political units, maybe yes. But we would preserve some of these and are providing for that in the scheme which we worked out in the Constitutional Commission. In cities of four or five members or even in counties with about the same number, is this really so? Especially where the boundaries are re-drawn and very artificially re-drawn every five or ten years. I believe that the whole city or county is a far more natural unit of representation.

However the multi-member constituency is not essential to a more proportional system. The additional Member System, or its Hansard Society modification, preserves the connection between the individual member and the constituency. Two-thirds of constituencies would be single-member units under the German system, three-quarters under Lord Blake's system.

I prefer the Single Transferable Vote (STV), in multi-member constituencies, but not passionately or overwhelmingly. The one, in my view, is about eighty per cent better than the present system and the other ninety per cent better. The difference is no greater than that.

We need and are mounting an all-party campaign. Let us cherish our courageous allies from outside the Alliance. It is relatively easy for us. It is more difficult for them in their party circumstances.

We can and must mount a major constitutional debate, comparable with the great reforming campaigns of the nineteenth century. It is for a great cause. It should not be presented in any narrow way. It is not for selfish ends. It is for fairness and the better government of this country.

European Voters have been cheated

On 25 July 1984 Roy Jenkins went to Strasbourg and in the European Parliament he and Madame Veil held a joint press conference advocating a fairer voting system. Here is the EEC press release on his contribution:

Britain's 'winner-takes-all' electoral system has cheated the voters of Europe.

Over two and a half million voters, 19.5 per cent of those who voted in Britain in last month's European elections, were not able to elect a single member of the European Parliament. Compare this to the Netherlands, where one million voters was sufficient to elect five Liberals. And in France, the governing Socialist Party got twenty seats with just over twenty per cent of the vote. 5.4 million voters in Britain have elected forty-five Conservatives, over 11.5 million voters in Italy only twenty-six Christian

Democrats. Such figures distort the entire political balance in the European Parliament.

The arguments for 'winner-takes-all' in European elections are even less convincing than in national elections, where no governing majority is at stake.

Under any system of proportional representation, the Alliance would have obtained fifteen seats and their failure to do so alters the balance in Parliament as a whole, added Mr Jenkins. It was no accident, he said, that the participation in Northern Ireland, where elections were held under a form of Proportional Representation, was twice that in the rest of the United Kingdom.

Mr Jenkins said that this would be the first of a series of visits to Europe by Alliance leaders to press the case for electoral reform.

Decentralisation of Government

During the course of the Hillhead by-election it was inevitable that Roy Jenkins should speak on the government of Scotland. Commentators had no idea how the new SDP would fare in a Scottish constituency. Previously the SDP had filled the role of providing an alternative to the large national parties. The SDP policy on this subject was, therefore, awaited with sharpened knives not only by the Scottish National Party (SNP) but also by the Labour and Conservative parties, each of which had foundered on their policies regarding devolution.

The speech that Roy Jenkins delivered at the Scottish Council for Educational Technology on 10 March 1982 went beyond the question of just Scotland and Wales: it spelled out the SDP policy on the major constitutional reform of decentralisation of government throughout the United Kingdom.

The Scottish people have every right to feel aggrieved about the treatment they have received at the hands of both Labour and Conservative parties over the crucial issue of the government of Scotland.

Although for many years past it has been the determined and settled view of a substantial majority of the people of Scotland that they should have a greater degree of control over their own affairs, the Conservative Party has consistently sought to make the minimal response to this demand which it judged necessary to retain its electoral support. Now that they are the Government, the pledges they gave in the run-up to the referendum on 1 March 1979 have been conveniently forgotten. The day before the referendum, on 28 February 1979, the *Scotsman* reported Mrs Thatcher as saying 'A "No" vote does not mean the devolution question will be buried'. In fact, there was a narrow 'Yes' vote but Mrs Thatcher has buried devolution anyway. There is clearly no chance of a constructive response to Scotland's aspirations from that quarter.

Nor can the Labour Party offer a convincing prospect of imaginative constitutional reform. Their favoured measure, the 'Scotland Act', received only lukewarm support in the 1979 referendum, with almost as many voting against. The clear message of that vote was that although the Act would have provided Scotland with its first elected Assembly since 1707, people were deeply unhappy and uncertain about the particular proposals which had been put to them. And they were right to be so, because the Scotland Act had not sprung from a settled conviction on the part of the Labour Party that decentralisation had become necessary for the good government of the country. On the contrary, the Labour Party was and remains a statist party with a profound belief in the achievement of its aims through vigorous use of centralised power. The Scotland Act was illogically cobbled together to serve short-term electoral purposes. And if in response to similar pressures in the future, the Labour Party were to decide once again to present a slightly different mix of *ad hoc* proposals to the Scottish electorate, these would be no more likely than last time to amount to a constitutionally coherent system of devolved government for Scotland.

Yet the evidence is that this is what the great majority of people in Scotland want. No more than a small minority are interested in separation: they wish to remain within the United Kingdom. They want more control over their own affairs, but they do not want a return to the Scotland Act. They want a new approach. My intention tonight is to set out what in my view the main lines of approach should be.

Let me say first of all that I do not believe that the case for a substantial decentralisation of power is confined to Scotland. Many of the ill effects of an over-centralised system of government are felt in Wales and the regions of England as well as in Scotland. That is why one of the themes repeatedly stressed by Social Democrats since the Party was founded has been the need to decentralise government to 'the nations and regions of Britain' as a whole. To say, however, that the establishment of a strong Scottish assembly should be seen as part of a general move to a more decentralised structure of government throughout the United Kingdom should not of course be taken to imply either that the devolution of power to Scotland should wait for developments in other parts of the United Kingdom, or that the scope of devolution to a Scottish assembly need exactly match the power given to regional assemblies in England. It will almost certainly be appropriate to invest a Scottish assembly with a

L

somewhat wider set of powers than those acquired by the English regions.

On what principles should a decentralised system of government be based? I described the broad objectives of what is now our policy in March 1976 in a speech in Inverclyde: 'a coherent and enduring constitutional framework which reconciles the legitimate demands for Scottish control over Scottish affairs with the equally legitimate requirements of democratic and effective United Kingdom government'. The Alliance is committed to the integrity of the United Kingdom, and our policy is to strengthen the political and economic unity of the Kingdom by establishing a successful and effective system of decentralisation. If, however, the new constitutional framework is to prove 'coherent and enduring', it must seek to embody three basic principles.

First, coherence. There must be a general principle against which the powers and functions appropriate to each level of government can be determined. I suggest as an axiom that no decision should be taken at a higher level of government which can with equal or greater effectiveness be taken at a lower level. (I use the word 'effectiveness' here so as to embrace consideration both of efficiency in execution and of success in matching measures to local aspirations.) This principle is sufficient to ensure real and genuine decentralisation, but it also places responsibility for whatever concerns the United Kingdom as a whole with the United Kingdom Parliament.

Second, we must seek to ensure the minimum political interference by the Westminster Parliament and Government with the new institutions. The transfer of power to Scotland should provide for the maximum freedom over what are properly regarded as purely Scottish affairs, and intervention by the Westminster Government should not be inconsistent with such a settlement.

Third, we must seek to establish arrangements which will minimise avoidable conflict between the different tiers of government. There are two main areas where conflicts are likely to arise — questions of *vires* and the allocation of finance — and we must ensure that there are workable and fair methods of settling conflicts in both areas. Some conflicts will be unavoidable but if we can regulate them adequately on the basis of my second and third principles, then — always assuming that our proposed constitutional arrangements command general support in the first place — we can have confidence in the stability of the new constitutional framework and in the continuing political and economic unity of the United Kingdom.

Lest anyone doubt the force of these principles, I should point out that their adoption would have precluded many of the provisions of the

Scotland Act. A concern to minimise conflict would not have allowed a block grant mechanism based on annual negotiations between the Assembly and London — a recipe for continuous argument if ever there was one. It would not have left the UK Government and Parliament with the unfettered power to overrule the Assembly on questions of *vires* instead of drawing on the independence of the judicial process. Concern for the second principle — minimising political interference from the centre — would not have permitted the House of Commons to retain the right politically to override the Assembly in any matter simply by virtue of its supreme legislative authority. Nor would it have allowed the Westminster Government in the last resort unilaterally to determine the finance available for the Assembly.

These then are powerful principles, and provide the basis for a new approach to the devolution of power, and a new and lasting constitutional framework. What sort of arrangements would be consistent with a determined application of these basic principles? What could the scope and powers of a Scottish Assembly be, and how would these fit in with the wider constitutional arrangements of the United Kingdom?

It almost goes without saying that the Scottish Assembly must be directly elected by a system of proportional representation. The first-past-the-post system — undesirable in the United Kingdom as a whole — would be unacceptable in Scotland where, with a four-party system, the relationship between seats and votes could allow the dominance of a caucus or a region. I am convinced that this was a major factor in the weakness of the 'yes' vote in 1979. The governing combination in the Assembly must represent a majority of the Scottish people, and changes in voting opinion must be accurately reflected in the Assembly so that it is properly responsive to the people it represents.

Turning to the functions of the Assembly, I propose that the Assembly should have substantial powers including legislative powers in all the major areas proposed for devolution in the Scotland Act — health, education, housing, roads and transport, agriculture and fisheries, water supply and sewerage, town and country planning, social services, tourism and so on. I would also make local government and local finance the responsibility of the Assembly. It would in my view be essential to accompany the introduction of an Assembly by the replacement of the existing two-tier local government structure with single-tier authorities so as to avoid over-government and excessive bureaucracy and expense. Exactly how this should be done — the redistribution of powers, the settling of boundaries and so on — would be a matter for the Assembly to decide. In addition, because of the unique position of the Scottish legal system, there is much to be said for a transfer to the Assembly of legislative control over Scottish private and criminal law, and control over the administration of justice and the prison service. By virtue of these matters alone, the range of functions which fell to a Scottish Assembly would necessarily be broader than those of English regional governments.

I propose, however, that in the context of the new constitutional settlement, the functions of the Assembly should extend well beyond the proposals in the Scotland Act in two important respects. First, it is clearly essential that the Assembly should have powers to enable it to guide and assist the progress of the Scottish economy. If the new constitution is to endure, the distribution of powers must broadly satisfy the aspirations of the majority of people, both as citizens of Scotland and of the United Kingdom. To establish an Assembly which was powerless to affect those matters of greatest concern to the people of Scotland would be a recipe for continued discontent and instability. Governments have held back from devolving economic powers in the past because they have used industrial and regional assistance on advantageous terms to attract mobile industry to depressed areas. There is, however, increasing evidence that these types of regional policy have failed. A new approach to development is needed.

In my view, the way forward is through a system of development agencies backed by sufficient powers and finance to help develop *indigenous* industry with long-term potential. One of the advantages of a regional tier of government in the UK would be the improved environment it would afford for the operation of regional development agencies like the Scottish Development Agency (SDA) (or better still Dutch Regional Development Companies) instead of the existing nationally organised grants system and the plethora of nationally-organised one-purpose agencies or arms of government (such as the Small Firms Centre) which we have at present. I envisage that the Agencies or Development Corporations should have wide planning powers, and access to finance on a sufficient scale to enable them to have a major impact on economic development by, for example, encouraging small businesses and locally based companies, assisting improvements in industrial efficiency, providing or co-ordinating provision of the infrastructure needed to support industrial development, and engaging in urban renewal and environmental improvements where these will aid development. In my view there should be such development corporations not only in Scotland and Wales, but also in the English regions. Within a general context of this type, I would not hesitate to give the Scottish Assembly control of the SDA and the Highlands and Islands Development Board — and indeed extend their scope in the ways I have indicated — to enable the Assembly to make a determined attack on the fundamental problems of the Scottish economy.

Second, I must say a word about the arrangements for financing the Assembly. I do not believe that the Assembly should receive its finance solely from a block grant negotiated annually with the Westminster Government. There will in any arrangement have to be a large grant element to ensure that each nation or region has sufficient resources overall to provide an equivalent standard of services. The basis for this grant should, however, be as objective as possible, based on a formula including the maximum of objective indicators, negotiated ideally between the Westminster Government and the nations and regions as a whole, and subject to revision not more frequently than every five years. In addition the Assembly should have a substantial revenue-raising power of its own. In my view, a substantial proportion of United Kingdom income tax should go to the Assembly from the day it is set up. There are no significant macro-economic arguments against a tax power provided that the Assembly has an obligation to balance its books: if expenditure and tax revenues rise and fall together, there should be no real headaches for the economic and monetary union.

The chances of continuous damaging friction between the Assembly and the Westminster Government would be much less under this financial system than under the Scotland Act. Annual negotiations would be avoided. The Assembly would be encouraged to act responsibly because it could be required to meet additional spending from its own taxation. The objectivity and infrequent negotiation of the formula, and the existence of a substantial tax power would have the further advantage of minimising conflict between Westminster and Edinburgh. It is a system informed by both the second and third of the fundamental principles I set out earlier.

I must finally mention two additional means by which I believe those basic principles will need to be safeguarded. First, the position of the Scottish Assembly and the regional assemblies *vis-à-vis* the central government will need to be safeguarded by giving them representation in the Second Chamber of Parliament. I envisage that one aspect of a reformed House of Lords would be a substantial element of national or in England regional members. This would in no way prejudice the continuance of directly elected Scottish Members of the House of Commons or the presence of the Secretary of State in the Cabinet.

One of their functions would be to scrutinise United Kingdom legislation to ensure that it did not unreasonably encroach on the areas intended to be within the competence of the assemblies. Second, we cannot allow questions of *vires* to be decided by the Westminster Government which will generally itself be an interested party.

Constitutional issues concerning the competence of the assemblies should be distanced from the reach of temporary political majorities by depending on judicial review rather than political override.

The constitutional proposals which I have set out are designed to provide the Scottish people with a system of government more effective in operation and more responsive to their needs and aspirations than either the present system or that proposed in the Scotland Act. I have proposed a powerful assembly, with substantial powers in all the major areas proposed for devolution in the Scotland Act, but with the economic powers, including revenue raising, to enable it to make a real impact on Scotland's economy. At the same time, I have proposed a set of arrangements designed to work smoothly and minimise the likelihood of conflict between the Assembly and the Government in Westminster, and to enable the Scottish Assembly to fit readily into a general system of decentralised government operating across the United Kingdom, if and when this comes into being. I have therefore sought to develop proposals for the decentralisation of power which will serve to fortify rather than undermine the essential unity of the United Kingdom to which I am wholly committed. No doubt the outcome in practice, like all human endeavours, will fall short of perfection, but in my judgement a constitutional reform of this type offers the best prospect of the coherent and enduring settlement which the majority of people both in Scotland and in England would like to see achieved, and which would underpin and not undermine the Union.

CHAPTER VI

How to win next time

Retrospect and Prospect

On 11 July 1984 Roy Jenkins gave the first of the Tawney Lectures at Bedford College, London.

My objective in this speech delivered three years after Warrington, the first election which the SDP fought, and four and a half years after the Dimbleby lecture, is to look back at some of the objectives of those ventures; to see how far we have achieved them; and to suggest ways in which we can make the full breakthrough which so narrowly eluded us in 1981-83.

I begin with an unashamed piece of nostalgia. I shall end more controversially. On this day in 1981 we had five days to go at Warrington. We still had no idea what sort of result we were going to get. We were sailing in an untested boat on an uncharted sea where the old navigational instruments did not work. It was, looking back, an even more extraordinary adventure than it seemed at the time. Despite the success of the launch of the party we were completely untried on the ground and in the polling booths. Warrington was one of the last seats we would have chosen to fight first. The Labour vote had been sixty-two percent of the total in 1979. There was only a Liberal vote of under 3,000 on which to try to build and, as became clear early in the campaign, even these exiguous few could not be automatically counted upon. An alleged Social Democrat had actually stood at that election and polled 144 votes. Any result between an humiliating fifteen per cent and what we actually got would have been a perfectly possible outcome. I think that right up to the moment when we went in to the half-completed count our best percentage guess was that we were somewhere in the low thirties. But it was all very uncertain.

We actually got 42.4 per cent, exactly, as it happens, the same percentage with which the Conservative Party won 396 seats in June 1983. We would have won with forty-four-and-a-half to forty-five per cent. Could we have done it? The margin sounds so narrow as to be easily bridgeable. Yet I rather doubt it. I think that in the circumstances of expectation we had squeezed out pretty well every available vote. A longer campaign would not have helped. What, however, I do believe is that, had the election been repeated, with people voting a second time, as in France, in the knowledge of how close we had come on the first occasion, then we would have won. When we toured the town on the morning after the result there were many more people who wished they had voted for us, many more even who almost believed they had, than had in fact done so.

Ought we then to have falsely proclaimed a conviction, which we did not have, that we would win? We never did. We said we would astonish the sceptics with the strength of our vote, but we did not go further. I think rightly, for two reasons. First the spirit of the SDP was to some substantial extent a revolt against the meaningless hyperbole of language which adversarial politics had encouraged. Not only was every opponent a scoundrel but he was certain to be trounced by the electorate. One of the purposes of joining the SDP was to be able to speak sense unmuzzled and not to have to repeat the claptrap which emerged from either side of Smith Square. It would therefore have been a pity to begin shouting exaggerated claims we did not believe. I think we should stick to this approach. We should be optimistic, but we should not lie.

The second reason was one of tactics not morals. Our realistic objective was to fire a shot from Warrington which would ring around Britain — perhaps some of the world as well. We had to put ourselves firmly on the electoral map. That is what we achieved. This did not however require an approach of win or bust. Indeed that would have been a great recipe for undermining the credibility of the infant SDP before it had even got going. What we needed was that the commentators and the public should express surprise at how well we had done. To have raised advance expectation of an unlikely victory would have been a self-inflicted wound.

For my second and last section of retrospect I turn to some more qualitative reflections on the nature and lessons of that campaign. There are three thoughts which particularly remain with me. First, it was surprisingly enjoyable. We had practically all the fun. The Labour candidate must have felt like someone on a supposedly impregnable bridge which begins to fall down, and the Conservative can hardly have been totally unaware that he was losing three-quarters of his vote.

My second thought bears on the discrepancy between the excellence of our Portsmouth performance and the disappointment of the Euro-election result. I believe that from Warrington onwards we have depended enormously on being able to establish direct personal contact with the electorate. This mainly means canvassing, but not just canvassing on the old pattern where you merely tried to find out where your support was and get away as quickly as possible. It means a conversation with the potential voters, in which their disillusionment

with the existing system is given time to surface. Public meetings are to a
substantial extent a substitute. They were, however, not so much a
feature of Warrington as of the Hillhead by-election. There we calculated
that we managed to address over a quarter of the total electorate in this
way, which must be a near record for any recent election. Either method
is clearly most possible in a concentrated by-election constituency and
least possible in a vast anonymous Euro-constituency. But before we get
too euphoric about this thought in relation to the fact that any further
Euro-elections are a long way off, and that our impending tests will all be
by-elections, we should remember that these are in a sense only training
exercises, even if with live ammunition, for the engagement which really
counts, which is the next General Election. And that has to be fought on
terrain which is as extended, although not as barren, as that for the Euro-
elections. And this will inevitably mean overstrained resources.

This brings me to my third Warrington reflection — on relations with
the Liberals. Although it had been assumed from the foundation of the
SDP, then only two-and-a-half months behind us, that we would work in
friendly association with them, there had hitherto been no opportunity
for practical collaboration. Nor had we worked out any terminology.
There was no mention of the word 'Alliance' in my election literature, nor
any joint logo. I described myself as 'Social Democrat with Liberal Party
Support'. There were not, to be honest, many Liberals in Warrington to
give any support. But nor, for that matter, were there many Social
Democrats in the town itself, although there was a good area party,
mainly in the surrounding suburbs and villages. However, Liberals, as
did Social Democrats, poured in from all over the country. Even the
'dreaded' Liverpool Liberals sent us several coach loads of skilled and
vigorous canvassers. We learned a lot from them about the techniques of
guerrilla politics without the resources of massed battalions and
traditional votes. There was practically no friction, as there rarely has
been on the ground. Nearly everybody enjoyed working together and an
essential paving role for the setting up of the Alliance in the Autumn was
performed.

Since then the continuing need for the Alliance has not been
challenged by the great majority of both parties. Disputes have been
about the allocation of seats, in the circumstances remarkably few, and
about the future relationship of the two parties. I will endeavour to give
my views about the last point in a series of fairly dogmatic propositions,
given in this form not because I wish to be dogmatic, but because to argue
them all out would take too long.

First, I have never had the slightest doubt that it was right to set up the
SDP as a separate party, although from the beginning envisaging re-
alignment and alliance. We were able as a new body to recruit most

valuable people both inside and outside politics for whom the skin of the old Liberal Party would have been too tight. Second, I do not however take the view that there are great ideological differences, still less, as some would have it, almost 'ethnic' differences between the two parties. Others may have sharper nostrils but I cannot instinctively tell a Liberal from a Social Democrat when I meet one in by-election committee rooms! Certainly the view held at one stage that we would be manifestly to the left of a centrist Liberal Party, and would consequently automatically have a greater penetration in Labour seats, while they might be the more effective challenge in Conservative held ones, is now manifest nonsense. There are of course differences within and between the two parties. We in the SDP are, I suppose, more naturally geared to government, although unless we emulate the feat of the Swedish Liberals who in 1978 managed to form one on the basis of thirty-nine seats in a Parliament of 349, we have some way to go before we again enmesh with it. But I honestly believe the Alliance is ideologically about as cohesive as any decent democratic grouping ought ever to be, substantially more so that either the Labour or Conservative parties.

Third, I do not believe that there is sense, even if we assumed electoral reform to be in the bag, which would be a very rash assumption, in envisaging a future for four independent main-stream groupings in British politics. We would make a great mistake if we gave the impression that our marriage with the Liberals was one of short-term convenience, and that if we ever felt free and strong enough to do so we would be off on our own. The Alliance in my view is 'for better, for worse'. There can be no SDP triumphs or defeats which are not also Liberal triumphs or defeats and *vice versa*. Nor can one party effectively immunise itself from weakness or instability in the other. Foolish policies adopted by one are a noose around the neck of the other. This will be even more true as we get to the threshold of winning a general election and have a sharper light of public scrutiny turned upon us. The way to avoid danger here is to work out a sensible joint policy together, and not to believe that one party can deny the sins of the other.

I believe that if this quasi-philosophical point about the full commitment to a joint common future is resolved then a lot of tensions are removed and a lot of problems fall into place. The detailed domestic arrangements can proceed without undue hurry or constitutional complication, and indeed to some extent piece-meal. Where on the ground people in both parties wish to be mingled together, let it happen. Where they wish to be somewhat further apart, there can also be local autonomy. But let no man seek to set a limit to the spontaneous moving together of an alliance. 'Let it roll', as Churchill, thinking of the Mississippi, said about Anglo-American unity in August 1940. 'Let it roll on in full flood, inexorable, irresistible, benignant, to broader lands and better days.'

My fourth and last point about relations with the Liberals is this. We are both of us thin on the ground for the manifold tasks we have to perform. The votes are there to be gathered in, but it is a labour-intensive job gathering them and we are short of hands. It is therefore essential that we do not waste the resources we have by overlapping, by trying to do the same job twice — or even three times — once in each party and once in the Alliance, and in consequence ending up with a great number of jobs not done at all . That is no way in which to perform the feat of political engineering, almost but not quite as difficult as the original launching of the SDP and the Alliance, which now awaits us.

The feat required is to maintain the purposes for which the SDP was established without inflicting upon the country, by default, by minority vote, a generation of Thatcherism. I echo Keynes's 1926 *cri-de-coeur*: 'I do not wish to live under a Conservative Government for the next twenty years.' I do it the more strongly because I regard Mrs Thatcher as much worse than Baldwin, and I think that she has set the Conservative Party on such a course that the probability is that her heirs and successors will be as bad as she is herself. I think that those who believe that a series of skids on banana skins is going to lead us straight back to what they see as the golden age of the third Marquess of Salisbury are deluding themselves.

There have been some ludicrous suggestions in the past few months that the SDP is on the way to becoming a sort of junior Thatcherite party. 'Not while I'm alive *it* ain't' as Ernest Bevin said about Aneurin Bevan being his own worst enemy. But happily the silliness of the proposition does not depend upon my prospects of longevity. The whole spirit and outlook of the SDP, its leaders and its members, is and must be profoundly opposed to Thatcherism. Our policy themes must always make this abundantly clear. I take four points to illustrate this.

First, there can be no question of our going along with the fatalism of this Government's acceptance of massive unemployment buttressed by de-industrialisation and the run-down of public services. Apart from anything else this policy will leave us in the most perilous state when the oil begins to run out. We must of course eschew any unrealistic promises that we can bring unemployment crashing down overnight, and recognise that there is a limit to what this country can do on its own. But quietism in the face of social disaster for millions of people and whole regions of our increasingly split nation we will not accept. We are not going to be refugees from the policy of rational expansion on which we fought the last election merely because we did not wholly succeed in getting the message over.

Second, I believe increasingly that our original SDP view in favour of a stability of frontier between the nationalised and the private sector is right. It was based on two premises: that ownership, provided it was not constantly changing, was not terribly important; and that kicking industries like footballs up and down the field, as in the classic example of steel, was highly undesirable for effective management. Anything that was done or undone was likely to be reversed within five or at most ten years. Today, compared with the time of the Dimbleby Lecture or Warrington, there is not much strength left in the pro-nationalisation team. But that does not change my view that government-induced changes of ownership, even if there is a reduced likelihood of their being quickly reversed, serve political dogmatism far more than they serve efficiency or the national interest. I would not rule out any change in any circumstances but I think that the onus of proof must be heavily upon those who want to make it, and I am certainly not prepared to chase off indiscriminately after the fashionable false god of privatisation, even when it is bedizened with the paint of proclaiming, mostly falsely, a better service to the consumer. Certainly no recent experience, either of selling of state assets or of the industrial relations performance of nationalized corporations, suggests that a change one way or the other is worth the candle.

Third, even after the Fontainebleau settlement, I remain profoundly suspicious of the ability of this Government to play an effective hand in Europe, or indeed, on arms control, or in relations with the Third World. Mrs Thatcher is of course right to want a fairer financial deal for Britain and a better balance in the Community budget between agricultural and non-agricultural expenditure. But she is profoundly wrong in thinking that this can be best achieved by the negative approaches of instinctive hostility to the build-up of non-agricultural Community activities, which inevitably cost money, and of clinging to the veto like a drowning woman to an oar. This is no way to exercise leadership, of which there has been a dearth in Europe for several years past, which could have been a great opportunity for Britain. But it has been missed. Such leadership as is re-emerging is once again Franco-German and not tripartite. Nor is a devotion to the right of any single country to block any proposal it does not like a good method for the promotion of British interests, let alone the wider ones of Europe. The free use of the veto in a Community of Ten, still more when it belatedly becomes one of Twelve, is a recipe for a frozen Community, incapable of substantial change or movement. As Britain desperately wants change, because the present shape of the Community, as we are constantly complaining, does not wholly suit us, we are perversely damaging our own interest. And as Europe, which has been bogged down and not seen a real initiative since the EMS five years ago, desperately needs movement, it is anti-European as well. And during this period of immobility and book-keepers' wrangling we have steadily lost ground vis-à-vis both the United States and Japan.

Mrs Thatcher, by her shrill chauvinism over several years, has created for herself a Frankenstein of anti-Europeanism on *her* wing of the Conservative Party. A high proportion of her strongest supporters have become raucous 'know-nothings' on Europe; and as her courage rarely extends to slapping the Tory Right, this makes her minimalist and therefore ineffective in Europe. It is part of a wide foreign policy gap between her and the Alliance.

Fourth, and of increasing importance, the SDP must be profoundly opposed to the increasing centralisation of power, which is an obsession of this Government and is beginning to lap, menacingly, against the outer walls of a fully plural society. This takes a variety of forms: the Cabinet, the Prime Minister apart, is the weakest and most centripetal I have ever seen. There is not a single Commons member of it, with the possible exception of Mr Prior who appears to be going, who has an independent reputation and who could not be got rid of more easily than Mr Murdoch or Mr Rowland could sack an editor. Lords Hailsham and Whitelaw certainly had such reputations, but they will not long preserve them if they go on acting as rather pathetic agents of what Lord Hailsham once nobly denounced as 'elective dictatorship'. What is certainly the case is that there is more talent and character amongst ex-ministers on the back benches than there is around the Cabinet table. They are excluded on grounds of ideology, not of ability. The Government in consequence is not merely unrepresentative of the nation. It is unrepresentative even of the forty-two per cent of the voters, thirty-one per cent of the electorate, who voted Conservative in 1983.

Nevertheless this increasingly narrowly based Government overrides local autonomy in a way that would be inconceivable in any other Western democracy, with the possible exception of France, which is in any event moving in the opposite direction. The right way to correct abuses in local government is by reforming the electoral system, which would avoid caucus control, and not by arrogating power to the centre.

At the same time there are, I believe, more political tests applied to public appointments than has ever previously been the case in this century. This applies to senior appointments in the civil service, to heads of major public bodies outside Whitehall such as the Bank of England and the National Coal Board, and to those charged with important *ad hoc* enquiries. I do not believe that the younger equivalents of Sir Michael Palliser and Sir Douglas Wass would today be appointed permanent secretary to the Foreign Office or the Treasury. I am convinced that no one has a chance of being appointed Governor of the

Bank who has views as independent of the orthodoxy of this Government, as, the other way round, were the views of those who served under Labour Governments in the forties, sixties and seventies. I am perfectly certain — to go back much further — that Mrs Thatcher would not today emulate Baldwin in 1925 and appoint the equivalent of Sir Herbert Samuel — Lord Grimond? — to conduct an enquiry into the coal industry. She will no longer even create life peers of independent eminence because of their regrettable propensity to vote against the higher lunacies of her Government.

All this is bad for the best traditions of independence of mind and fearless advice of the civil service, and bad also for the quality of government, particularly with a self-righteous Prime Minister of narrow if firm judgement, surrounded by a weak Cabinet of her own creatures.

All these undesirable tendencies must be strongly opposed by the Alliance. The gulfs between us and the present Government are many and wide. We want to get rid of it at the earliest possible moment. I do not however believe that the way to do this is to seek an alliance, 'rainbow' or otherwise, with the Labour Party. With Mr Frank Field, as of course with Lord Young of Darlington, one of the most creative innovators in Britain, I could be happily part of any grouping. But going over the rainbow with Mr Kinnock or Mr Hattersley would be a very different matter. To be fair to them, I do not think they would have any desire to do so with us. They are far too frightened by their own embittered and exclusive militants, and in a sense they are quite right for there is hardly a single major issue of politics on which we agree with Labour Party Conference decisions. Maybe they do not always themselves, but Mr Hattersley is too supine to say so and Mr Kinnock is too verbose to be understood. However, it leaves us in a modified Groucho Marx position. He did not want to join any club which would have him as a member. The club we do not want to join is one which would not want us as a member. So the proposition is in any event unrealistic.

This does not mean that we shall not welcome ex-Labour votes whether they come to us tactically or, better still, with full conviction. But let us not be in any doubt that it is the forty-two-and-a-half per cent of Tory votes, and particularly the first-time Tory voters of 1983 and 1979, many of them having switched straight from Labour, which are the most vulnerable and desirable *cache*. They would be so for the Labour party if that party showed any signs of a real long-term revival, but in my view it does not. The uplift they secured as a result of Mr Kinnock's election barely carried them over a few months. But these votes are substantially available to the Alliance. In Portsmouth we mostly made them stay at home. In future we must get them to come positively to us.

We do this neither by proclaiming a false willingness to sustain a

Labour Government, even if we kept it in chains, nor by adopting a sub-Thatcherite posture, least of all at the moment when both her style and her substance are beginning massively to alienate the electorate. We will do it best by underpinning the Alliance and by sticking to the principles and policies on which we were founded and on which, from Warrington to Portsmouth, we have fought with a much greater degree of success than I dared to hope four-and-a-half years ago. What we need now is steadiness of nerve, consistency of purpose and more committed workers on the ground. They are not impossible requisites. With them we can, at the second run, make a reality of the great prospect which opened up before us in 1981.

Other books published by
THE RADICAL CENTRE

CALLING THE SOVIET BLUFF
by Nora Beloff

NEITHER HAWK NOR DOVE: A *THIRD* APPROACH TO
ISSUES OF SECURITY
by Ronald Higgins